CW00468290

DIPLOMAT WITH A DIFFERENCE

Peter,

I hope you enjoy it.

Greetings.

Roy

DIPLOMAT WITH A DIFFERENCE

Roy Dean

ARTHUR H. STOCKWELL LTD
Torrs Park, Ilfracombe, Devon, EX34 8BA
Established 1898
www.ahstockwell.co.uk

British Library Cataloguing-in-Publication Data.
A catalogue record for this book is available
from the British Library.

To Heather,
my heroic mainstay through
troubled times.

ISBN 978-0-7223-4258-9
Printed in Great Britain by
Arthur H. Stockwell Ltd
Torrs Park   Ilfracombe
Devon   EX34 8BA

CONTENTS

FOREWORD

I wish I had a mind like Roy Dean's. Here is a man who can do the *Times* crossword while he boils his breakfast egg – he has twice won the national championship; who has *invented* such new verse forms as the clerick, the trimerick and the decouplet ('Go and catch a falling star | Who's had too many at the bar'); and – most remarkable of all – who can compose a perfect impressionist word-picture in seventy-two consecutive palindromes. I would give a lot to have written that superb parody of one of Cole Porter's best songs, which includes the immortal quatrain:

> *You're the pits,*
> *You're a running eyesore,*
> *You're the spits*
> *On the streets of Mysore*

or, better still, Roy's addition to *A Shropshire Lad* ('In spring the hawthorn scatters'), which waits till the very last line for its punch. I have read it dozens of times in public; it never fails to raise a deafening guffaw from the audience.

I could go on, but why read me when you can read Roy? I can only suggest: if a man with a brain like that finds himself as acting British High Commissioner in Ghana, could he have been wasting his time?

John Julius Norwich.

PREFACE

A paperback edition of *Mainly in Fun,* a collection of my writing in prose and verse over a period of fifty years, with a complimentary foreword by Colin Dexter, appeared in 2002. Its humour has amused countless readers, but it has been out of print for some time.

Now, at the age of eighty-five, suffering from a rare combination of Alzheimer's and Parkinson's, I thought I had better launch another book while I still have some faculties left. The present compendium is not only a memoir of my diplomatic career, but it also brings together a number of monographs, verses and articles on various subjects of interest to me, written since my retirement from the diplomatic service in 1987. I hope it will give the reader some of the pleasure I had in writing it.

Roy Dean, Bromley, January 2012.

INTERNATIONAL AFFAIRS

In 2008 I was invited to give a talk to the Bromley branch of the U3A on life in the diplomatic service. I wanted to avoid the dull details of official procedures, and to concentrate on more-interesting aspects. My talk, built around a series of anecdotes, was intended to show how the use of words and music can have some unusual influence on diplomatic relations, both bilateral and multilateral. The following memoir is based on that talk.

DIPLOMAT WITH A DIFFERENCE

When you read or hear the words 'British diplomat' what image comes to your mind? Probably someone tall, of impressive appearance, from a good family, with a first-class university degree, well spoken, well dressed and with a rolled umbrella, having social skills, and possessing a keen intellect, excellent judgement and political acumen. I was none of these things, so how did I end up in the diplomatic service?

It's a long story. I was born in a Watford council house in 1927, with tubercular neck glands. TB was rife among poor families at that time, and often fatal, but somehow I survived. My first recollection is of lying in the sun on a hospital balcony. I had an elder sister and brother. My father was a railway signalman earning £2 a week, and to pay the rent my parents took in lodgers, so you can imagine how cramped the accommodation was.

Because of my illness I didn't start full-time education until I was seven. Until then, I learned at home with my mother. There were no books in the house, so I read a daily paper, and that helped me to study various styles of writing and to build up my vocabulary. At my primary school there were fifty children to a class, but the teaching was good, and at the age of eleven I won a scholarship to the local grammar school.

My sister and brother were both working in factories, and their wages bought me a pair of black shoes and a second-hand school uniform in which the shorts didn't quite match the jacket. This made me the object of some ridicule at first, but I quickly, discovered that the best way to gain acceptance and popularity was to use humour, sometimes at others' expense.

I joined the school's Air Training Corps squadron in 1941 and my ambition was to get into the RAF. I volunteered on my eighteenth birthday and took my medical at Stanmore RAF station, but was told to stay at school to get my Higher Certificate, for which I gained distinctions in French, German and English literature, and qualified for a State Scholarship.

The war ended suddenly before I could join up, and I didn't get into uniform until October 1945, when I enlisted in the RAF Volunteer Reserve. I then spent the next two years doing clerical work in station headquarters at several airfields in India, defending the North-West Frontier against Afghan marauders. It was rather like a modern version of *Carry on up the Khyber.* I was demobbed in 1948, and went back to the family home with demob suit, raincoat, shirt and underwear.

University was out of the question; I was living in my parents' house, and I had to get a job to support them. I heard that there might be a vacancy at the Building Research Station, an outpost of the Department of Scientific and Industrial Research within cycling distance of my home. I had a short interview there and was hired as a temporary clerk grade 3 (the lowest form of life in the civil service).

The registry was like a Dickensian office. In charge was a higher clerical officer sitting on a dais. The huge amount of incoming correspondence was handled by three clerical officers who entered the papers, put them into a file and sent them to the appropriate scientist to be dealt with. When action was completed, the files were placed in a large wooden box in the middle of the room. My job was to collect them and put them back where they belonged in large racks.

However, my RAF service entitled me to take the Civil Service Reconstruction Examination for the executive class, which I scraped through seventy-ninth out of eighty. I was asked which government department I would like to work in. I opted for the Central Office of Information (COI), which had succeeded the wartime Ministry of Information. I was allocated to the Magazines Section of

Publications Division, and from being a callow, unworldly youth I became overnight a publishing executive at a salary of £265 per annum, working on a chain of pocket magazines in six languages, similar to those dropped over occupied Europe during the Second World War.

The Treasury put a stop to that in 1951, and I moved to the home desk, providing material for the wide range of public-information campaigns then emanating from Whitehall. At the same time I realised that I needed some qualifications, so at evening classes I acquired diplomas from the London College of Printing and Graphic Arts (book and magazine production) and the College for the Distributive Trades (advertising and public relations).

In 1955, now married, I, was promoted to information officer, and did some interesting things with public-service adverts on prevention of accidents in the home, to fill the vacant slots of the Independent Television companies which had arrived in 1956. But by 1958 I was tired of working on domestic campaigns and wanted to spread my wings, using my communication skills.

At that time more and more British colonies were becoming independent, and the Commonwealth Relations Office (CRO) was setting up diplomatic missions around the world. Each high commission had an information section, which seemed appropriate for me to apply for. There was no examination for this service, just an interview in which I made the most of my experience at the COI and my professional qualifications (which were probably rare in a potential diplomat).

I passed, and was delighted to be seconded to the CRO as second secretary (information) at our high commission in Colombo, a post which required communication skills rather than political acumen. Heather, my wife, liked the idea of an overseas posting and gave up a well-paid job with an advertising agency to accompany me.

Heather and I knew that the best way to obtain favourable publicity was to be visible, vigorous and versatile. Although a junior member of the staff, I had a wider range of Ceylonese contacts than my colleagues, thanks to my customers in the news media. Above all, I felt that cultural diplomacy was the best way to win friends and influence people.

We were given a splendid house and garden, in which we regularly used to entertain our Ceylonese guests. We started by showing a documentary film about Glyndebourne opera in the garden after a buffet supper, and scored a direct hit with a clever young journalist who had an influential column in the *Ceylon Observer*. He wrote us up and continued to report my public activities. All the papers printed more of my press releases as time went by.

Similarly, Heather was interviewed in the *Times of Ceylon* about her career as a book editor and public-relations executive. We quickly became the best-known diplomatic couple in Ceylon. Quite against the rules on working wives, I helped Heather get a job as film reviewer for Radio Ceylon. Friends in India who heard her broadcasts were amazed!

We were advised to join the Queen's Club in Colombo, but on being taken there we were appalled to see only white faces! It was almost like a hangover from colonial days. We preferred to join the Ceylonese 80 Club, where we mixed with politicians, senior civil servants, artists, writers and journalists.

We toured the island extensively, often with a lawyer friend in Kandy who was equally proficient in Sinhala and Tamil, and when I gave a talk he would translate into those languages. We stayed on tea estates with our Ceylonese friends and visited all the fine antiquities in what was then a veritable tropical paradise.

In 1959 Earl Attlee, who as Britain's prime minister had granted Ceylon independence in 1948, was invited to the island to give a lecture on 'Constitutional Government'. As the junior member of the British High Commission I was appointed his 'minder'. I was absolutely thrilled because he was my greatest political hero; during his administration between 1945 and 1951 I had served firstly in the RAF in India and then in the COI working on government information campaigns.

I called on him at his hotel and asked whether there was anything he would like.

He replied, in his famously laconic manner: *"The Times –* crossword and cricket scores."

I explained that the paper arrived daily in the unclassified bag, and undertook to extract it for him. He was most grateful, and I retain in my mind's eye the picture of him happily puffing away on his pipe as he solved the puzzle (at which he excelled).

When Aldous Huxley visited Ceylon in 1961 I happened to be at Ratmalana Airport seeing a couple of young journalists off to the UK when his aircraft landed. A bevy of local reporters wanted to interview him, and naturally I was glad to arrange it for them. As a result of this a photo of me with Huxley and his wife appeared on the front page of the evening paper.

My high commissioner, an erudite musicologist, was furious, because he had hoped to meet Huxley himself. I was summoned to his office and given a severe dressing-down. I didn't actually mind because I was only doing my job, and Huxley was a great writer. I had asked him what he considered to be his most satisfying work, and he told me *Time Must Have a Stop*.

A golden opportunity for publicity came when the MCC team under Ted Dexter were to visit Ceylon in 1962. It occurred to me that all their names could be the subject of puns – *dexter*ity, and so on. I wrote an 'Ode to the MCC' in this style, which my friend on the *Ceylon Observer* printed in his popular column.

A Ceylonese rhymester liked it so much that he responded with an 'Ode to the Dean'. This had an amazing effect in a cricket-mad country. My poem was reprinted as a valedictory when we left the island in 1962 – Heather was expecting her first child, a son born in Hampstead shortly after our arrival.

On my return from secondment I officially transferred to the Commonwealth Relations Office. Our next posting, to Vancouver on the west coast of Canada in 1962, was not so enjoyable – it really was the end of the line at that time, though it is now a bustling cosmopolitan city. Victoria, the capital of British Columbia on Vancouver Island, was a delightful place to visit, and I tried unsuccessfully to interest the local officials in a hovercraft service which would avoid the hundreds of floating logs in the Pacific Strait. Fortunately my promotion to first secretary came though in 1964 and we were able (now with two small boys) to resume our travels.

This time it was to Lagos, then the capital of Nigeria. As first secretary (information) I had to put out a daily service of press releases on aspects of Britain and its policies, which were widely printed in the Nigerian papers. I also produced a quarterly magazine called *Insight*, designed to convey subtle propaganda for British achievements, institutions and culture, which had a commercial sale of 7,500.

One serious problem we faced was the Nigerian Government's reaction to Britain's apparent unwillingness to sort out the colonial situation in Rhodesia. One morning in November 1965 I was listening to the BBC World Service over breakfast when the news bulletin opened with a bombshell: Ian Smith, Prime Minister of Rhodesia, had issued the country's unilateral declaration of independence (UDI).

Taking office in 1964, Smith had rejected British terms for independence which required moves towards black majority rule, and African politicians had been imprisoned. Negotiations with Smith led by the British prime minister, Harold Wilson, on the basis of a biracial compromise had broken down. But because Britain was not in a position to use force against the government of Rhodesia, a landlocked country, most African leaders were convinced that the two prime ministers were colluding in preserving white minority rule in that country. To African leaders, UDI would be the final proof of British duplicity; we could expect the anger of their people to turn to anti-British violence as Africa felt betrayed.

Driving straight to the office, I asked the political officers in the Chancery if there had been any guidance from the Commonwealth Relations Office on handling UDI, and what official statement we could put out to the people of Nigeria showing the British Government's opposition to Smith. There was none – other than that UDI was illegal.

Immediate action was essential as my daily press bulletin had to reach newspapers and other media offices by 10.30 a.m. The only solution, was to concoct a statement based on what I thought the British Government might be considering. Using the heading 'Britain Vows to Bring Down Smith', I drafted a list of measures including economic sanctions (such as import and export bans, an embargo on the supply of arms and foreign exchange and travel restrictions) and other actions we would undertake, with the support of other Commonwealth countries, to isolate the Smith regime and bring about its downfall. Naturally the measures were not specific and had no time frame.

By 10 a.m. the release was on its way to all the national media in Lagos. The next morning I was relieved to see that the leading government newspaper had reproduced the press release on its front page with my title as a huge banner headline. Other media had also given it favourable coverage, though not as forcibly.

Meanwhile reports were coming in about demonstrations against British embassies and high commissions all over Africa, often culminating in hostile crowds putting our offices under siege, with the tacit compliance of their governments. Some British Council centres were attacked and destroyed. But, mercifully, none of our diplomatic missions or cultural premises in Nigeria was harmed.

Our third son was born in 1965 in the Shell/BP clinic in Port Harcourt – the centre of Nigeria's offshore oil industry, in which the British company had a major interest. But this became a difficult post in 1966 when the prime minister and members of his government were assassinated in a military coup. In 1967 the Eastern Region seceded from the federation as 'Biafra', and the civil war began.

A skilled and unscrupulous public-relations agency in Geneva, probably financed by our commercial rivals, put out a daily tissue of lies that succeeded in convincing the world media that the conflict involved the Muslim majority in the north suppressing the Christian minority in the east. Consequently the myth of 'brave little Biafra' won many supporters, including a group of Conservative Catholic MPs who engineered frequent debates in Parliament, which were so widely reported that Britain was thought to be supporting the rebels in Nigeria. The federal government was ill-equipped to counter this propaganda, and it fell to us, with the aid of our defence advisor, to brief the large contingent of British correspondents in Lagos on the realities of the situation.

The scene was further complicated by the BBC Overseas Service, which insisted on giving both sides of the conflict – facts reported by their own experienced correspondent in Lagos and fiction from a freelance reporter in 'Biafra' – quite often in the same news bulletin! We felt powerless to protect our diplomatic relations with a friendly Commonwealth country. It was a relief to leave Nigeria when our tour of duty ended.

While we were in Lagos, Branches A and B of the foreign service, the Consular Service, the Commonwealth Relations Office's political and information wings, the Trade Commissioner Service and the rump of the Colonial Office had been amalgamated into Her Majesty's Diplomatic Service. This meant I could now serve anywhere in the world and do any job – but having entered the new organisation through the back door, with no time for diplomatic training in Whitehall, I would now be in competition with the most experienced members of the service. What hope did I have of advancement in this field? I could only do so by using my initiative.

At the end of 1968 I took over a desk in the Disarmament Department of the Foreign and Commonwealth Office (FCO), with the task of getting the Nuclear Non-Proliferation Treaty (NPT), signed in July 1968, ratified by the forty-three states needed to bring it into force.

The UK, USA and USSR, as 'depositary powers' of the treaty, worked together in this joint enterprise; we once met in the Soviet Embassy in Vienna. The UK canvassed its Commonwealth partners, the USA its allies, and the USSR its satellites. I sent instructions to our high commissions with background on the treaty and the kind of arguments that might be deployed in persuading their host countries to ratify it.

I particularly wanted the Vatican on board, and when we achieved this the Holy See opened diplomatic relations with the Kremlin so that Cardinal Casaroli, the Pope's Foreign Secretary, could go to Moscow to ratify the treaty.

The first obstacle was that the Americans counted the ratification of Taiwan, which we and the Russians did not recognise, and the Russians counted East Germany, which we and the Americans did not recognise. While the superpowers were level in numbers, the UK was one behind. The solution (which the Americans called 'The Dean Plan') was for a bunch of states to ratify on the same day, so that we three passed the post together. It all came good on 5 February 1970 with impressive ceremonies in our three capitals. Many more states have since ratified the

NPT, but regrettably India and Pakistan, among others, have not.

The year 1970 was really my annus mirabilus. In the same week as the NPT ratification, my family moved from a small townhouse in Beckenham to a Victorian villa in Bromley, with ample room for three boys and a French au pair, and a spacious garden.

During the summer *The Times* staged the first National Crossword Championship, in which 20,000 competitors took part. After regional heats eliminated most of them, 300 were left to face the final at the Europa Hotel on a warm August weekend.

By a great stroke of luck I won the trophy. My photo appeared on the front page of *The Times* on the Monday, and that morning I was photographed by the *Evening Standard* solving the *Times* crossword on the train up to Victoria. In the evening I was interviewed by Jonathan Dimbleby on BBC Television News.

The next day I received a personal letter from the Foreign Secretary, Sir Alec Douglas-Home. He wrote:

> Many congratulations on winning the Crossword Championship.
> I knew there were many quick-witted and well-read people in the Service but it was good to see this widely advertised in the papers yesterday.

The *Times* championship, being a unique event, had worldwide coverage and gained me an entry in *Who's Who*, giving unexpected momentum to my career. The FCO's personnel department considered where to post me so that my spurious fame would be of maximum value to Britain's diplomatic and commercial interests.

I was sent on an economics course at the Civil Service College. This was not only a valuable education in itself, but provided the stimulus for my satire on professional methodology and jargon entitled 'Academics and the Keynesian/Friedmanite Controversy' – the fiscal policies advocated in the UK by John Maynard Keynes versus the monetarism favoured by Milton Friedman of the Chicago School. This spoof paper included a diagram of the 'Theory Preference Curve', which purported to prove that the views of the economics professor at the Open University in Milton Keynes were probably paramount. My genial tutor, Professor Harry Johnson at the LSE, liked the idea and tried to get it published in an academic journal, but without success.

In 1971 the FCO decided to send me to the Consulate General at Houston, Texas. The previous system of separate commercial and information roles had apparently not worked, and FCO inspectors decided they should be combined.

Once again fortune was kind to me. The 1972 edition of *The Guinness Book of Records* had just appeared and the publishers put out a press release about six new entrants. My record for the fastest verified solution of the *Times* crossword was one of them, and when I arrived in Houston the local media queued up to interview me. Americans may not have been familiar with the cryptic crossword, but they liked the idea of having a world champion in their midst. Wherever I travelled in my parish of six south-west states – roughly the size of Western Europe – I was given access to the local press, radio and TV stations.

This gave me an opportunity to bang the drum for Britain's achievements, policies, goods and services. I spoke to Chambers of Commerce and Rotary Clubs, organised 'British weeks', and wrote an article for the DTI's *Trade & Industry* journal setting out the opportunities for British exporters in the south-west, which led to a significant increase in UK trade missions coming to Houston.

To publicise British products I used stunts like riding a shopping tricycle down Main Street in Houston and arranging a 'Picnic on the Bayou' to show off our finest antiques and reproduction furniture. The top department store re-enacted the Battle of Waterloo between astronauts and RAF war-gamers.

I liaised with the American oil companies who were setting up operations in Scotland for the North Sea oil-and-gas industry, and negotiated with a local firm to take over the troubled Upper Clyde Shipyard. I persuaded British firms to take part in Houston's annual Offshore Technology Conference, where they secured valuable contracts, particularly in the servicing of the oil rigs and drilling platforms. Business travel between Aberdeen and Houston increased dramatically.

On the cultural front, I was invited to open the annual Shakespeare season at the Globe of the Great Southwest in

Midland/Odessa, and an exhibition at the Presidential Museum in San Antonio on the first seven American presidents – who had all been British subjects! I visited the Alamo and was made an 'honorary admiral of the San Antonio River', which entitled me to commandeer any vessel on that water – though I never tried to. During the 'Festival of Romance' at a Houston store the local TV station obtained a number of UK programmes and for two weeks became 'The English Channel'.

In two years UK exports through the ports of Houston and New Orleans, which had been stagnant, increased by 25 per cent, and the UK became an important oil and gas producer. But I fell out with my boss over the unequal division of labour within the office. This was an unforgivable offence, viewed by the FCO as a 'personality clash', and in 1973 I was recalled to London.

I took over the desk in South Asia Department handling our economic relations with the Indian subcontinent. The first thing I did was some research into the figures of our trade with those countries. Analysis showed that our exports to India were not doing as well as they should, given the close historical and commercial links between our two countries, and the size of our aid programme to India.

I suggested that trade relations would benefit from the formal framework of an economic cooperation agreement. Talks were held with Indian officials, terms were drawn up, and in January 1976 I travelled to New Delhi with Peter Shore, the Secretary of State for Trade, for the official signature of the agreement (which has helped two-way trade to flourish).

We were cordially received and entertained by our Indian counterparts. The Indian Government and people had not forgotten that it was a Labour government in Britain in 1947 that had granted India independence with a parliamentary system of government – the largest democracy in the world.

But it was some time since a British cabinet minister had paid an official visit to New Delhi, and naturally Peter Shore wished to call on Indira Gandhi and discuss India's progress. However, there was a problem. It became clear that, whereas the Indian prime minister would have been glad to meet her British opposite number, in accordance with strict protocol she would not be able to see a mere trade minister.

I discussed the problem with her private secretary, an old friend from his days at the Indian High Commission in London, when we found we had a common interest in E. M. Forster. He knew that Mrs Gandhi liked to do a cryptic crossword, and mentioned to her that I was the *Times* champion. Incredibly, for one so preoccupied with affairs of state, she agreed to see me.

Thus it came about that I was ushered into her sanctum for a chat about our shared interest, with my minister waiting in the wings. She told me she liked to relax with a crossword at the end of the day, while I preferred to tackle one early in the morning to sharpen my mind. We discussed the types of clue that we enjoyed. I was privileged to have a most interesting conversation with Mrs Gandhi for ten minutes.

As I thanked her for her kindness, I asked her if she would like to meet Mr Shore, who was in the room next door.

"Of course," she replied.

The ice having been broken, our minister was invited to pay a courtesy call on her. I shall never forget the look on his face as I beckoned him in! He was able to conduct his official business in a very useful meeting which helped to reinforce UK/India relations at the highest level.

As a result of this episode, later in 1976 I was appointed director of the FCO's Arms Control and Disarmament Research Unit (ACDRU), a small academic section responsible for formulating UK proposals in the various international negotiations. Part of my job was to improve public understanding of the efforts being made to achieve arms-control agreements, which were hardly ever mentioned in the British media because they lacked news value.

At the height of the cold war it also became necessary to counteract the KGB's flood of propaganda and misinformation which had stirred up fierce public controversy about nuclear weapons throughout Western Europe since 1978.

In a speech on 6 October 1979 President Brezhnev claimed that the proposed deployment by NATO of ground-launched Cruise and Pershing II missiles would upset an existing parity in East/West intermediate-range nuclear forces (INF), increase the likelihood of a nuclear war limited to Europe, give the United States the ability to launch a 'first strike' attack against the Soviet Union, and make European states accepting them a target for Soviet nuclear weapons.

These arguments – though palpably false – were calculated to alarm the populations of Western Europe, to fuel the movement for unilateral disarmament by the West, and to disguise the fact that the Soviet Union had been installing its multiple-headed SS-20 missiles targeted on Western Europe since 1977. And, most crucial of all, they largely ignored NATO's simultaneous commitment to engage in talks on limiting INF, and the importance of the proposed deployments in persuading the Soviet Union to negotiate on mutual reductions.

This negative propaganda was immediately successful. Widely disseminated by the KGB and other Soviet organs, such as the World Peace Council, it produced a climate of opinion that completely dominated the public debate. The misinformation was accompanied by a cynical Soviet 'peace offensive'.

But the greatest change in public attitudes after 1979 was that uneasiness about the *possession* of nuclear weapons was replaced by sharper concern about their use. It was this fear of nuclear war that inspired the huge public protests which were a political and social phenomenon of the 1980s. Fanned by the KGB, fear became the mainspring of the movement for unilateral nuclear disarmament by the West. In Britain, for example, the KGB London Residency boasted in June 1982 that it had brought a quarter of a million people out on the streets in a protest demonstration.

In my view, the principles of nuclear deterrence, carefully formulated and mutually accepted by politicians, military leaders and defence strategists, were not understood by the general public. Here Western governments had been at fault; no effective action had been taken over the years – possibly through a concern that this might somehow reveal aspects of NATO's nuclear strategy – to inform their populations how deterrence had worked and how successful it had been in keeping the peace in Europe. Hence the doctrine that nuclear weapons were not for *fighting* wars but for *preventing* them had never been accepted by the anti-nuclear campaigners.

The KGB could call on an elaborate machine for disseminating cold-war propaganda; the NATO countries were slow to react. When they eventually did so, the most urgent task was to inform their publics of the real facts about disarmament.

I put forward a proposal for a thirty-two-page quarterly newsletter giving details of the ongoing international negotiations, the British Government's policies, speeches by ministers in the Geneva Committee on Disarmament and the United Nations, and important statements in Parliament. With the approval of Douglas Hurd, the incoming Minister of State, this publication, called *Arms Control and Disarmament,* started in August 1979 and quickly attained a circulation of 5,000 among lecturers, journalists and many non-governmental organisations.

On the personal side, 1979 was also memorable for the arrival of a beautiful daughter, and a second victory in the *Times* National Crossword Championship. This was held at a time when the paper was not being published; consequently the event was taken up by other British media and the world press.

The newsletter was augmented in the run-up to the Second UN Special Session on Disarmament in 1982 by an information pack consisting of a leaflet clarifying the nuclear debate, an educational wallsheet and a booklet, *Peace and Disarmament,* the introduction to which was reproduced in an English textbook published by Edward Arnold as an example of a piece of prose clearly explaining a difficult subject to the public.

I also used these publications in a presentation at NATO Headquarters in Brussels for information officers from member governments, which resulted in the adoption of a common policy, with some of the material being translated into other languages.

It is unusual for a British diplomat to operate publicly in the UK, but in this instance I was given a free rein by my minister to carry out an information campaign. I contributed numerous articles to learned journals, particularly those of the Royal Institute of

International Affairs, the International Institute of Strategic Studies, the Royal United Services Institute for Defence Studies, NATO and the UN.

These were widely read and sometimes reprinted elsewhere. Their impact was reflected in a personal attack on me in the official Soviet journal, *International Affairs,* and a very complimentary profile by Peter Hennessy in *The Times* headed 'Wise Owl Watches the Doves and the Hawks'! A Dutch newspaper printed a similar article calling me 'Mr Disarmament'.

Briefings were given to diplomatic correspondents and Church leaders, papers were presented at NGO seminars in Britain and to the UNESCO Conference on Disarmament Education in Paris, and lectures were delivered at the international-relations departments of several universities. The thrust of the argument was that negotiated measures for mutual weapons reduction were the best recipe for world peace. As unilateral disarmament was challenged, a more sensible debate emerged.

In May 1982 President Reagan announced that the United States was putting to the Soviet Union a practical plan for the phased reduction of strategic nuclear weapons. He proposed that the bilateral Strategic Arms Reduction Talks (START) should begin by the end of June 1982. Shortly afterwards I received a visit from two counsellors in the Soviet Embassy who wished to talk about START.

Their main question was could the United States really be genuine in wanting to reduce nuclear weapons to the extent outlined in President Reagan's plan? I assured them that this plan had been seriously conceived and, coming from a Republican administration, would carry great political weight in the US Senate. My advice to them was to take up this offer of deep cuts from President Reagan, for they were unlikely to get a better opportunity. My visitors duly made notes and presumably reported back to Moscow. The talks began in 1982 and resumed in 1983, but proceeded slowly, with several interruptions. START I was signed in 1991 and START II in 1993.

In 1980 the UN Secretary General had set up an Expert Group on Disarmament Institutions, to make recommendations on how the existing international machinery could be improved to speed up negotiations. The Group of Twenty-One was to present its report to the Second UN Special Session on Disarmament in 1982.

I was nominated the UK representative on the group, most of whom were members of their countries' missions to the UN and lacked real expertise on the subject. Our chairman was the Argentine Ambassador to the UN.

The group eventually split into three factions on lines of national interest. The first consisted of the United States and the Soviet Union combined with their allies; the second was a non-aligned section to which France attached itself with its usual astute tactic of winning friends; and the third was the small remainder, including me. I had no official remit; my main aim was to get some discussion going on the international trade in conventional arms (which had cost millions of lives since the end of the Second World War).

The United States and the Soviet Union did not wish other states to get involved in the intricacies of nuclear disarmament. They therefore tended to block any initiatives from the non-aligned group. It became clear that we should have trouble in reconciling differences between the two major factions.

Things were reaching an impasse when the first draft of the report was tabled; each recommendation was scrutinised in detail and rejected by one or other of the two sides. So I decided to adopt an independent stance and play the honest broker. Taking into account the wide gap at the outset, I tentatively suggested a compromise wording to which all parties would have no objection. Our chairman seized on this as the middle way that would cut down the discussion and enable us to proceed.

If any paragraph was hotly debated he would say, "Perhaps we could ask the British representative to suggest a form of words."

Scribbling furiously, I did as he requested.

The final report presented to the UN Special Session on Disarmament in 1982 may have done some good through its recommendations in areas other than the bilateral nuclear-disarmament negotiations, but I was unable to get any movement on the conventional arms trade because of opposition from the non-aligned countries, who were the major recipients of these weapons for their own defence.

Before the UN special session Pope John Paul II had written to the heads of government of the nuclear-weapon states asking them to set out their policies on nuclear disarmament. His letter to the British prime minister was passed to me for a draft reply.

It seemed to me that this was a perfect opportunity to explain in non-technical terms Britain's objective of securing the multilateral reduction of nuclear weapons through serious international negotiations. I drafted a carefully worded statement along these lines and submitted it to Number Ten. Mrs Thatcher approved it and her reply was sent to His Holiness.

In his message to the UN special session in June 1982, Pope John Paul II called for 'negotiations leading to a reduction of armaments that is balanced, simultaneous and internationally controlled'. I could not have wished for a better outcome.

After my NATO presentation I was invited to Washington in November 1982 for a meeting with officials in the State Department, Department of Defence, Arms Control and Disarmament Agency and US Information Service. Although I was a fairly junior diplomat, they believed me to be of senior rank and listened attentively. I spoke quite strongly about recent statements by President Reagan on 'limited nuclear war' which had alarmed the people of Western Europe and were in stark contrast to Brezhnev's 'peace offensive'. I argued that a more balanced response was needed, and that a statement by the US president on protecting peace would help to reduce the influence of 'the anti-nuclear protesters'. Fortunately he did this two weeks later.

The principal effect of the anti-nuclear campaign in Western Europe had been to encourage the Soviet Union to stall for some two years in the INF negotiations that had been initiated in 1981 on the basis of NATO's twin-track proposals for mutual reductions. It was not until the first deployment of the NATO missiles took place in 1983 that these talks began in earnest.

With Gorbachev's arrival negotiations were speeded up and in December 1987 the United States and the Soviet Union signed an INF agreement in Washington providing for the global elimination of American and Russian ground-based missiles with a range between 500 and 5,000 miles. The removal of Cruise missiles from Britain followed shortly afterwards under a phased programme between the two sides. Ironically, the Greenham Common protesters claimed this as a success for their campaign!

It had taken eight years to accomplish our aim – the first international arms-control agreement to abolish a whole category of nuclear weapons. But the result fully justified the effort and it had an even greater significance in bringing East and West into dialogue instead of confrontation, and thus hastening the end of the cold war.

Meanwhile I had been promoted, and in December 1983 I was posted to our high commission in Accra, the capital of Ghana, as counsellor (economic/commercial). In effect, I was deputy high commissioner. Shortly afterwards the high commissioner (an old friend from Colombo days who had actually met his future wife at our house) went on leave and I assumed charge. I shall always remember the feeling of pride the first time I was driven out in the official Range Rover flying the Union Jack, and policemen in the streets saluted.

My first assignment was to address the annual meeting of the Ghana Manufacturers' Association (GMA) on the subject of 'small industries'. The DTI sent me some background material on how small firms in the UK were encouraged through the establishment of industrial estates and science parks. In my talk I was able to emphasise the importance of small businesses to the national economy, in Ghana as well as the UK. My talk was put out by the GMA and later published in one of the UN economic journals.

But I was immediately faced with a crisis. We were building a splendid new office to accommodate the various sections of the high commission, and the foundations had already been laid by Taylor Woodrow at great expense. The chairman of the ruling Provisional National Defence Council (PNDC) was J. J. Rawlings, a flight lieutenant in the Ghana Air Force, who had been imprisoned for opposing the previous corrupt government. This had been overturned by a military coup in 1981 and, released as a national hero, he had taken over the reins of office. However, some anti-British elements in the PNDC now claimed that our new office was in a residential area and had no planning consent. The police moved in and the site was closed off. I asked my staff for the relevant documents, and was horrified to see that there was just a piece of paper signed by a junior official.

My only hope of retrieving the situation was to get the head of state to countermand the closure order. I telegraphed the FCO and asked for the Minister of State, Malcolm Rifkind, who had met Rawlings, to send him a personal letter explaining the importance of the office to diplomatic relations between our two countries. This letter arrived in the bag on Thursday.

I had secured an audience with the Chairman on the Friday afternoon, and went along with my defence advisor, a Falklands veteran, armed with the letter, architect's plans and an artist's colourful impression of the completed site. Chairman Rawlings read the letter, studied the plans and said he would look at the site himself and give me his decision. An official from the Foreign Ministry called at my house on the Saturday to say that the Chairman had agreed the plans, subject to some minor changes. I immediately telegraphed the good news to the FCO.

I had no acknowledgement from the political desk in West Africa Department, but at the next meeting of the EU heads of mission at my house (the UK was then in the presidency chair) members were generous in their congratulations on a diplomatic coup. The US Ambassador called to say how impressed he was by this success. British firms – especially Taylor Woodrow – were similarly delighted.

At a national ceremony soon afterwards, Chairman Rawlings approached me with a smile and asked if I was pleased with his decision. I assured him that it would be of great benefit to both our countries. Two weeks later I signed the first UK/Ghana Economic Aid Agreement.

After a bad road accident in August 1984 in which my boss's wife and driver were killed, and he and his three children were seriously injured, he was flown to London and I became Acting British High Commissioner for a total of one year. I was also deputy high commissioner, counsellor (economic/commercial) and head of Chancery. Combined with all my representational duties, this was a heavy burden, particularly as I was on my own, running a large house with eight servants, ordering food and drink supplies from a London agent, and entertaining on a considerable scale. And because the office had no central structure, every member of staff reported direct to me; my door was always open.

We were also the British Embassy for neighbouring Togo. As this was a Francophone country I was required to take the intermediate French examination before I paid my first visit there in 1984. This came at an awkward time; the scion of an influential English family had drowned off the coast at Lomé in mysterious circumstances. As I had to stay in constant contact with the FCO, which was under great pressure, I sent a member of my staff to Lomé to investigate and report back. The Alliance Française arranged for me to take the four-part exam in my office, in two hours rather than the scheduled three. I was quite surprised that I passed with a mark of 76 per cent.

I then made periodic official visits to Lomé. For example, in 1984 I escorted a group of four British MPs (including Clement Freud), who were reciprocal guests of the Togolese National Assembly, in a call on President Eyadéma, and in 1985, when the London-based Inter-Parliamentary Union (IPU) held its annual meeting in Lomé, I acted as guide for a group of sixteen officials and MPs for several days. We had a very entertaining evening at my favourite restaurant, Les Relais de la Poste.

Troops from Ghana (then the Gold Coast) had fought for Britain in two world wars, and great importance was attached to the Remembrance Day ceremony in Black Star Square, for which stands were erected for ministers, diplomats and the general public. In 1985 my defence advisor and I were among the Commonwealth diplomats laying wreaths.

Without any preparation, we instinctively marched in step, side by side, up to the memorial, halted, bowed, saluted, laid our wreaths, executed a smart about-turn and marched back to the diplomatic stand, to huge cheers from the crowd.

The US Ambassador leaned forward and murmured, "You British do this so well!"

Trade promotion then occupied more of my time. In September

1986 I was present at the signature of three large contracts won by British exporters, totalling £35 million. The managing director of one company thanked me for my efforts with the chief secretary and remarked that without my intervention the contracts would have fallen through. Official trade figures in 1987 showed that Ghana had become the third largest market for British exports in sub-Saharan Africa. Our aid programme was taking shape, and when Heather, who was now head of publicity at the Overseas Development Administration (ODA), paid an official visit to our aid projects in 1985 we had an unforgettable experience: a deep descent down the Ashanti Goldfields' mine at Obuasi.

As for cultural relations, I worked closely with my British Council colleague to increase the supply of books to school libraries which had become decimated over the years while Ghana had a severe shortage of foreign exchange. I presented equipment to hospitals, instruments to a youth orchestra, and 2,000 pairs of football boots which I am told were crucial in raising Ghana's performance in the international arena.

The director of the Arts Council of Ghana became a good friend and invited me to her events, at which I was usually the only diplomat present. I opened several art exhibitions in the splendid British Council Hall in Accra, and was cajoled into taking the part of Oliver Twist's grandfather (very poorly) in its production of *Oliver* there. One of my Ghanaian friends jokingly dubbed me the 'non-acting' high commissioner.

The British Council Hall was the major auditorium for musical and dramatic events in Accra. When the US Embassy hired it for a concert by the famous American jazz pianist Memphis Slim in 1985, I was so struck by his performance that during the interval I jotted down the lyric of a New Orleans-type twelve-bar blues on the back of my programme and showed it to him. He then gave an impromptu rendering of it, citing me as the most impressive collaborator he had ever had. This incident found its way into *Good Morning, Africa,* a popular BBC Overseas Service programme presented by Hilton Fyle, which was listened to by a large audience in Ghana. A government minister even rang to congratulate me on my musical prowess!

As time went on, I got to know Jerry Rawlings quite well. When Heather came out in the summer of 1986 we were invited to the Chairman's box at the annual race meeting and spent a very pleasant afternoon with him. The next day, at the annual government reception for the diplomatic corps, when heads of mission and their spouses lined up to shake hands with the head of state, Heather wasn't with me because she had had to return to her desk in London.

Jerry Rawlings looked puzzled and asked, "Where is she?" so she must have made an impression!

Just before I left Ghana, my old colleague John Julius Norwich was interviewed in the *International Herald Tribune* about his forthcoming *Christmas Cracker*. He generously spoke of my crossword record and called my seventy-two-line palindromic poem a work of genius. A friend in the US Embassy passed the cutting to a female reporter on the *Daily Graphic*, who had the bright idea of pitting me against Azumah Nelson, the world featherweight boxing champion. We met at the Accra Stadium and compared notes. My record for solving a *Times* crossword was three minutes forty-five seconds, but Azumah had knocked out his opponent in two minutes fifty-six seconds, so we agreed that he had won on points.

This was of course featured in the paper the following day, with a splendid photograph showing paper and pen versus boxing gloves. On the following Saturday morning an official from the Foreign Ministry called at my residence to say I was wanted at the Castle (the seat of government). For a diplomat to be summoned like that usually means bad news, and I was prepared for the worst.

Imagine my surprise when I was ushered into the presence of the head of state and his chief minister. They greeted me warmly, and mentioned that they had seen the newspaper report. They were impressed by my appearance in the record book, which they took to be a sign of high intelligence. Chairman Rawlings went on to ask whether I could offer any advice on how his government could improve the lot of the Ghanaian people.

Taken by surprise, the only suggestion I could make was that because the ruling PNDC was not recognised by some states, it might be a good idea if elections were held in which he and his colleagues would be democratically elected, thus legitimising his government in the eyes of the international community. This would pave the way for potential donors to provide economic aid to Ghana. In saying this I was sticking my neck out, but the reaction was friendly, and we parted on the best of terms.

(In 1992 elections were held and Jerry Rawlings was elected President of Ghana, an office which he occupied for two terms. The Queen paid a highly successful visit to Ghana in November 1999, and President Rawlings was entertained at Buckingham Palace in 2000.)

When I said goodbye to Ghana in December 1986, the British business community (mostly banking, insurance, construction, mining and transport) gave me a splendid lunch as a tribute to my work on their behalf.

Then a senior member of the government hosted a farewell dinner at a Chinese restaurant in Accra – a unique honour for a foreign diplomat.

Asked to say a few words, I said, "I shall always be grateful for the warm friendship of the Ghanaian people, at every level, that has made my time here so enjoyable."

This went down well, and a number of friends came to the airport to see me off.

I retired from the diplomatic service in February 1987 in the rank of assistant undersecretary of state. I was delighted when the Foreign and Commonwealth Office Association (FCOA) of retired diplomats was formed by David Burns in 1999 – a brilliant idea enabling us to keep in touch with former colleagues.

Once we leave the diplomatic-service list we tend to disappear from sight, with only a *Who's Who* entry to reveal our whereabouts. It has given me enormous pleasure to meet old friends and to make new ones at many of the interesting events organised by the FCOA Committee. I've also had the privilege of contributing the 'Diplodocus' crossword in each issue of that excellent magazine *Password*.

People sometimes ask me why, after such a busy and productive diplomatic career, I was never given some honour. A possible reason is that throughout my career I ignored the rule book (which I had never seen) and used unorthodox methods to achieve results.

33

Traditionally, a diplomat is judged by the quality of his reporting on political developments in the country he serves in. That was never part of my portfolio.

I was regarded as a person full of clever ideas, but not a team player, a loose cannon who occasionally embarrassed the FCO by taking initiatives without official sanction.

I often disobeyed Talleyrand's advice to his diplomatic staff: "Above all, gentlemen, not too much zeal."

I was regularly marked in 'box 3' of my annual confidential report.

Strangely enough, my work was more highly esteemed outside the service, both at home and abroad, than by my masters. But my satisfaction in having done a good job for my country – politically, culturally and commercially – was reward enough.

TIRELESS AMBASSADOR
(A Dramatic Fragment of Diplomatic Life)

Act I, Scene I: A diplomatic mission in Africa. An AMBASSADOR addresses his minions.

AMBASSADOR: So meet we here to make a true report
Which shall acquaint our officers of state
With late intelligence of dire events
In this unruly land.

(Enter a SECOND SECRETARY)

SECRETARY: What tidings, sirrah?
My Lord, I come in haste from far Magamba,
Whose dusty streets now flow with lanced blood.
'Tis said the ballot hath been foully rigged;
The politicians have deceived the people,
Who now avenge themselves. In wildest rage
They seize their masters and dismember them
With hissing matchets, limb from bloody limb.
Meantime th' opposing party, hopes frustrate,
Hath armed its thugs for battle. Shrieking hordes,
Drunk on raw spirit, leap into the fray
And plunge the country into hideous war.
I fear no aid can come from the militia
In such a pass. 'Tis each man for himself,
And devil take the hindmost. Yesternight
The maddened rabble took a deadly toll
Of mammy wagons on the motor roads;
Each highway now is choked with smoking cars
Whose ruins reek of human flesh. In short,
We are beleaguered.

AMBASSADOR: We thank thee for thy pains.
An MBE shall be thy just reward.
Now set the printer to its magic work,
And let the winged messages go forth
With most immediate speed. Nothing encypher,
But let the language speak both plain and frank,
Telling the tale before this day be o'er,
That sleepy clerks residing in Whitehall
Shall know what monstrous happenings befall.

Exeunt omnes.

This letter, sent to The Times *on 9 January 2003, was not printed. It was eventually published in* Password *in 2008.*

THE WRONG TARGET

There is a state in the Middle East that possesses weapons of mass destruction, illegally occupies territories in defiance of long-standing resolutions of the United Nations Security Council, deploys massive military force indiscriminately against a civilian population, and has killed over 2,000 men, women and children (including UN relief workers and foreign journalists) in the past ten years.

Yet immediately after taking office in January 2001 (after a fraudulent election victory) President George W Bush went out of his way in his first foreign policy statement to praise the Israeli Government and to castigate the Palestinian Authority. There is documentary evidence to show that he was acting on the advice of his Republican colleagues that this was the best way to win back the Jewish vote from the Democrats.

But it was a serious blunder. It is quite possible that this was a contributory factor in motivating Al-Qaeda to strike the US mainland through the September 11 attack on the World Trade Centre eight months later. In other words, Bush created the 'Terror' that he then declared war on.

The present Israeli Government continues to do its utmost to sabotage the Middle East peace process begun by President Clinton. With its cruel expansionist policies it represents a greater threat to world peace than Saddam Hussein. This judgement is based not on bogus "intelligence" but on facts.

Far from preventing terrorism, a senseless war against Iraq would provoke terrorist reprisals internationally on a scale that could hardly be imagined, with Britain a major target. We should be taking the lead in tabling a new resolution in the UN Security Council calling on Israel to return to the Middle East peace process, with the stated aim of establishing a viable independent Palestinian State.

In 1995 I joined the Biggin Hill Branch of the RAF Association and became its honorary press officer. The three pieces that follow were published in Air Mail *magazine.*

VICTOR IN THE BATTLE OF BRITAIN

2010 marked the 70th anniversary of the Battle of Britain. Fought in the skies over Southern England from June to September 1940, it ranks in our country's history with Trafalgar at sea and Waterloo on land.

The Royal Air Force was greatly outnumbered at the time by the Luftwaffe, many of whose fighter and bomber pilots had combat experience going back to the Spanish Civil War in 1936. Fighter Command did, however, have a remarkable leader – Air Chief Marshal Sir Hugh Dowding, a master of strategy whose brilliance won the Battle and saved Britain from invasion.

Dowding knew from intelligence reports of the modernisation and massive build-up of Nazi air power, and was aware that it was only a matter of time before an air attack was launched against the United Kingdom. From his office at Bentley Priory he fought tirelessly with the politicians and Air Ministry officials to speed up the production of Hurricanes and Spitfires to replace the outdated aircraft of the RAF. With phenomenal foresight, he also planned a detailed strategy to meet the threat of enemy attack.

On 24th May 1937 he delivered a lecture at the RAF Staff College: "Employment of the Fighter Command in Air Defence", expounding the threat and the measures being taken to counter it. The text of his lecture, with his own manuscript additions and amendments, was shown to me by his daughter-in-law, my old friend Odette, Lady Dowding. To my knowledge, it has not been published.

It is of particular interest to compare Dowding's 1937 lecture with his lengthy despatch describing how the Battle of Britain was actually fought and won, submitted to the Secretary of State for Air on 20th August, 1941. In it he paid a sincere tribute to the tactical skill of Air Vice-Marshal K R Park, who commanded 11 Group and has now been honoured by a statue in Waterloo Place.

70TH ANNIVERSARY OF
THE BATTLE OF BRITAIN

The 70th anniversary of the Battle of Britain, in which Biggin Hill had been the hub of our air defences, was celebrated with a commemorative event in Bromley on 25 June 2010 paying tribute to the 544 RAF pilots who fought and gave their lives in 1940.

Five of the surviving pilots, all in their nineties, arrived in a Vintage Vehicle parade led by 228 (Bromley) Squadron of the Air Training Corps, and were introduced and cheered by a huge audience.

Senior officers from the RAF and Air Forces of Australia, Canada, USA, Poland, Czech Republic and France were among the crowd who watched the BoB Memorial Flight flypast. 54 white doves were released in memory of the fallen. The vehicles then ferried the pilots and dignitaries to St George's RAF Chapel of Remembrance at Biggin Hill for a Veterans Day Service.

Dame Vera Lynn was the guest of honour at the buffet lunch which followed in marquees on the airfield, arranged by the organisers of the Annual Air Show that took place that weekend.

On 18 July a Service of Dedication was held in St George's RAF Chapel to mark the replacement of the Gate Guardians – the memorials to aircrew who died flying from Biggin Hill. The new Guardians are replicas of a Spitfire K9998 QJ-K of 92 Squadron, flown by Pilot Officer (later Squadron Leader) Geoffrey Wellum DFC, and Hurricane P2921 GZ-L of 32 Squadron flown by Flight Lieutenant (later Air Commodore) Peter Brothers CBE DSO DFC and Bar, who sadly died in 2009. An aerial display by two real aircraft made a fitting accompaniment to the installation of the new Gate Guardians.

St George's RAF Chapel of Remembrance at Biggin Hill was the scene of two splendid services on Sunday, 12 September to mark the 70th anniversary of the Battle of Britain 1940. Early in the morning the BBC's mobile recording crew arrived to tape the 8.10 a.m. Act of Worship broadcast on Radio 4 to a national audience.

60TH ANNIVERSARY OF HISTORIC RAF CHAPEL

On 17 July, 1951, Air Chief Marshal Lord Dowding laid the foundation stone of the rebuilt St George's RAF Chapel of Remembrance at Biggin Hill.

On Sunday, 17 July 2011, a Service of Evensong was held to celebrate the 60th anniversary of the Chapel.

The Anglican Official Chaplain was The Reverend Chris Baker, and the Preacher The Reverend (Wg Cdr) Richard Lee RAF (Ret'd). The Director of Music was Dr. Helen Isom and the Organist Paul Isom.

The service opened with the Introit sung by the choir: "Christ is our Cornerstone", by David Thorne. After the Old Testament reading from Job, Chapter 38, the choir sang the Magnificat to a setting in G by C. V. Stanford, followed by the Gloria. The New Testament reading was from Matthew, Chapter 21, verses 12–16. The choir then sang Stanford's setting of the Nunc Dimittis. Prayers of intercession were led by the Chaplain, and the address was given by Revd Richard Lee.

The guest of honour was Odette, Lady Dowding, who had presented the Chapel with the trowel used by her father-in-law in laying the foundation stone and "topping out" in 1951. It now lies in a glass case in the Chapel.

This article was published in Quest *in 2010.*

ENGLISH IN THE EUROPEAN UNION

When the 27 leaders signed the European Treaty in Lisbon in 2008 it was evident that few of them were able to sing the words of the EU anthem, Schiller's "Ode to Joy", because the majority could not speak German.

An obvious solution to this problem would have been to produce an English version which all nationals could sing. Perhaps some use could be made of the following translation, made in the same metre and rhyme scheme.

> Joy, thy godlike radiance spreading,
> Daughter of Elysian line;
> Drunk with rapture, we are treading,
> Sacred one, thy holy shrine.
> Let thy spell unite all others
> Rent apart by worldly things,
> All mankind becoming brothers
> Sheltered by thy gentle wings.
> May our millions be surrounded
> By this universal love!
> Brothers – in the stars unbounded
> Our dear Father reigns above.

Rather awkward, but then Schiller's dense style is notoriously difficult to translate. However, my proposal was taken up by Martin Lindsay, an English opera/lieder singer based in Cologne. In July 2012 he got a chance to sing my 'Ode to Joy' at the graduation ceremony of an American university in Luxembourg. He told me it went down very well, so let's hope that it catches on!

THE ART OF VERSE PARODY

The Concise Oxford English Dictionary defines 'parody' as 'an imitation of the style of a particular writer, artist or genre with deliberate exaggeration for comic effect'. But, rather surprisingly, parody does not earn an entry in *The Oxford Companion to English Literature*, and very few parodists are quoted in *The Oxford Dictionary of Quotations*. This seems rather a pity, because in its verse form it is a legitimate and enjoyable literary device. In preparing this paper I am indebted to G. H. Vallins, the Chaucerian specialist, for some of the ideas in his *Sincere Flattery* (Epworth Press, 1954).

The first essential element for the successful verse parodist is a really sound knowledge of poetic technique. He must be a finished and experienced craftsman with an ear for metrical and rhythmical effect.

Craftsmanship, then, will set him on his way. It will enable him to make humorous play with the form of his original, to produce easily recognisable burlesque, and pleasantly to kindle the laughter of his readers. But the true parodist goes deeper; he travesties *spirit* as well as form. His attitude is not only humorous, but also critical.

Criticism is the second great essential for the parodist, and the finest of English parodies are criticisms too. They take just those tricks and mannerisms to which the mind and metre of the poet are subject, and by magnifying them hold up to his style a magic mirror.

Lewis Carroll's parody of Isaac Watts's 'Tis the Voice of the Sluggard' is funny, but it concerns itself with form only. He goes much further in his 'You Are Old, Father William', where he derides the very spirit of Southey's unctuous platitudes.

And if we need a supreme example of the parody that is also criticism, we can find nothing greater than the Wordsworthian sonnet by James Kenneth Stephen in his 'Lapsus Calami' of 1891:

Two voices are there: one is of the deep;
It learns the storm-cloud's thunderous melody,
Now roars, now murmurs with the changing sea,
Now bird-like pipes, now closes soft in sleep:
And one is of an old half-witted sheep
Which bleats articulate monotony,
And indicates that two and one are three,
That grass is green, lakes damp, and mountains steep
And, Wordsworth, both are thine: at certain times
Forth from the heart of thy melodious rhymes,
The form and pressure of high thoughts will burst:
At other times – good Lord! – I'd rather be
Quite unacquainted with the A.B.C.
Than write such hopeless rubbish as thy worst.

So the parodist must be both craftsman and critic. But two more qualities are still necessary. The first is, quite simply, poetry itself. The true parodist is himself something of a poet. He has the poet's love of beauty and subtlety of insight. Without these things he remains a craftsman only.

Yet the craftsman/critic/poet of whom the parodist is all compact needs one final gift – that generous appreciation which is akin to love. In effect, the parodist is paying a form of homage to the poet.

As the seventeenth-century poet Edmund Smith wrote: 'To write lofty burlesque the author must be master of two of the most different talents in nature: admiration and laughter.' It is these elements that distinguish parody from satire, which sets out to be cruel and destructive. It is just because of this ability to blend admiration and laughter in their art that the great parodists have made no enemies.

The first notable English parodist was John Philips, whose *The Splendid Shilling* (1701) in the style of Milton was hailed by Addison as 'the finest burlesque poem in the English language'. Philips admired every word Milton wrote, and was able in a supreme degree to combine both admiration and laughter. His poem created for the art of parody a finished technique and inspired a host of imitators. But it was only at the close of the eighteenth century and the beginning of the nineteenth that the art of parody reached for a while its peak. In 'Progress of Man' (1798) John Hookham Frere, MP and diplomat, parodied Erasmus Darwin's 'Loves of the Plants'. His delightful mimicry includes one of my favourite couplets:

> The feather'd race with pinions skim the air –
> Not so the mackerel, and still less the bear!

He also worked with George Canning in producing 'The Anti-Jacobin' in 1798. Canning is perhaps the finest example of the parodist who probes to the very heart of his original and exposes spirit even more than form. His art gains, too, by the fact that he is statesman and politician as well as writer and critic. His immortal 'Needy Knife-Grinder' mocks poems by the lugubrious Southey and the political and social attitude of mind of the English Jacobin Party.

After 'The Anti-Jacobin' there comes yet another supreme achievement in the field of parody: the *Rejected Addresses* of Horace and James Smith. Drury Lane Theatre had been burnt down in 1812, and the committee offered a reward for a suitable address for its opening ceremony after the rebuilding. So the brothers hit on the wonderful idea of publishing the addresses *rejected* by the committee. They managed to parody all the great Romantics and their contemporaries, weaving each poem around some incident of the theatre fire. The best is their Scott, which relates in the narrative style of 'Marmion' the fates of two gallant firemen who wrestled with the flames.

The next great parodist is James Hogg, the Ettrick Shepherd. His *The Poetic Mirror,* published in 1816, was the amusing result of the refusal by his distinguished friends to contribute to a book of poems he was planning. He decided to produce the book himself, parodying not only his defaulting contributors but also himself. All are delightful and instinct with poetry and criticism.

Early in Victoria's reign a witty pair of writers, William Aytoun and Theodore Martin, took advantage of the interregnum on the death of the Poet Laureate, Southey, in 1843 to produce in 1845 the *Bon Gaultier Ballads,* a batch of 'Poems Forwarded to the Home Secretary by the Unsuccessful Competitors for the Laureateship'. Their Wordsworth sonnet was so good that many readers did not recognise it as a parody at all.

So we come to the greatest among the parodists of Victorian days, Charles Stuart Calverley (1831–84), a barrister of the Inner Temple who turned to poetry after a serious skating accident. His famous *Fly Leaves*, published in 1872, puts him on a par with those great Victorians with a genius for nonsense writing. His Browning version, called 'The Cock and the Bull', reveals that close and loving study of the original's style without which the great parody cannot be written. But his easiest subject to imitate was Jean Ingelow, a poet hardly remembered today, whose besetting sin was the use of flowery rhymes and archaisms.

J. K. Stephen (1859–92), whose Wordsworth we met earlier, was a cousin of Virginia Woolf. He was called to the bar, but devoted most of his time to journalism and humorous verse. Like Canning, he had the peculiar ability to explore the heart and mind of his original. His 'Walt Whitman' is an absolute hoot.

A great poet parodist, Swinburne, comes into the late nineteenth-century group. His self-parody, 'Nephelidia', is brilliantly done in its handling of language, alliteration, rhyme and metre to create a dreamy atmosphere. It begins like this:

From the depth of the dreamy decline of the dawn through a notable nimbus of nebulous noonshine,
Pallid and pink as the palms of the flag flower that flickers with fear at the flies as they float,
Are they looks of our lovers that lustrously lean from a marvel of mystic miraculous moonshine,
These that we feel in the blood of our blushes that thicken and threaten with throbs through the throat?

Swinburne himself was the subject of several parodists, notably Arthur Clement Hilton (1851–77), whose superb 'Octopus' was published in a Cambridge magazine in 1872. The promise shown by this young writer was destined never to reach fulfilment, for he died while still a very young man. I particularly like the last stanza:

> We are sick with the poison of pleasure,
> Dispense us the potion of pain;
> Ope thy mouth to its uttermost measure,
> And bite us again!

We then come to that clever parodist of the later nineties Sir Owen Seaman, editor of *Punch* and prolific author of light verse. He, like Bon Gaultier in the 1840s, seized on an interregnum in the laureateship created by the death of Tennyson, and filled the gap with his *Battle of the Bays* parodying Kipling and lesser contemporary poets. His 'A Birthday Ode to Mr Alfred Austin', the pedestrian laureate elected in 1896, is a masterpiece of banality. Its thirty-five verses open with:

> The early bird got up and whet his beak;
> The early worm arose, an easy prey;
> This happened every morning of the week,
> Much as today.

Moving into the twentieth century, one of the best of the earliest parodists was Sir John Squire (1884–1958), editor of the *New Statesman* and the *London Mercury*. In his excellent collection *Tricks of the Trade* he devotes himself to the ancients equally with the moderns. In doing so he evolved a new and intriguing technique, rewriting the products of one poet in the terms of another.

G. K. Chesterton (1874–1936) took up the challenge with his 'Variations on an Air', composed on having to appear in a pageant as Old King Cole. His Yeats parody is a masterpiece:

> Of an old King in a story
> From the grey sea-folk I have heard,
> Whose heart was no more broken
> Than the wings of a bird.

As soon as the moon was silver
And the thin stars began,
He took his pipe and his tankard,
Like an old peasant man.

And three tall shadows were with him
And came at his command;
And played before him for ever
The fiddles of fairyland.

And he died in the young summer
Of the world's desire;
Before our hearts were broken
Like sticks in a fire.

A Poet Laureate who was also a mischievous parodist is Sir John Betjeman. His 'Hymn' (1931) is a clever take on Wesley's 'The Church's One Foundation':

The Church's Restoration
In eighteen-eighty-three
Has left for contemplation
Not what there used to be.

Betjeman himself has been parodied. Perhaps the finest is Gavin Ewart's 'John Betjeman's Brighton'. He sets the scene in that Regency resort, and describes its denizens and the range of entertainments offered. Here is the first verse:

Lovely in the winter sunshine lies the Haslemere Hotel,
Near the Homeleigh and the Sussex, home of ex-King Manoel.
Lager in the West Pier Tavern, cocktails in the Metropole,
Who can spot Lord Alfred Douglas – not the gross and coarse of
    soul!

Alan Bennett has visited Metroland in an expert excursion into sewerage, 'Place-Names of China'. He starts vigorously with:

> Bolding Vedas! Shanks New Nisa!
> Trusty Lichfield swirls it down
> To filter beds on Ruislip Marshes
> From my lav in Kentish Town.

However, after enumerating the sanitary ware and its varied uses, his parody inevitably ends in a mood of melancholy:

> Here I sit, alone and sixty,
> Bald, and fat, and full of sin,
> Cold the seat and loud the cistern,
> As I read the Harpic tin.

Hugh Kingsmill (1889–1949) was an all-round man of letters: anthologist, biographer, literary critic, novelist and parodist. Michael Holroyd wrote a critical biography of him in 1964 and edited an anthology of his work in 1970. I love his brilliant 1933 version of Housman's *A Shropshire Lad*:

> What, still alive at twenty-two,
> A clean upstanding chap like you?
> Sure, if your throat 'tis hard to slit,
> Slit your girl's, and swing for it.
>
> Like enough, you won't be glad,
> When they come to hang you, lad:
> But bacon's not the only thing
> That's cured by hanging on a string.
>
> So, when the spilt ink of the night
> Spreads o'er the blotting pad of light,
> Lads whose job is still to do
> Shall whet their knives, and think of you.

Housman himself said: "This parody of me is the best I have seen, and indeed the only good one."

Similarly, T. S. Eliot is said to have enjoyed Henry Reed's inspired 1946 parody called 'Chard Whitlow (Mr Eliot's Sunday Evening Postscript)':

As we get older we do not get any younger.
Seasons return, and today I am fifty-five,
And this time last year I was fifty-four,
And this time next year I shall be sixty-two.
And I cannot say I should care (to speak for myself)
To see my time over again – if you can call it time . . .

The art of parody continues to be encouraged by literary competitions in the *New Statesman* and *The Spectator*. Many of the prizewinners, among whom Martin Fagg and Stanley J. Sharpless stand out, appear in a marvellous anthology edited by E. O. Parrott, *Imitations of Immortality* (Penguin, 1987), which includes prose as well as poetry. I myself have won a few prizes, starting with 'Ballade of Dead Poets' in 1951, and including 'Lovelace Bleeding' in 1986, which Colin Dexter used as a chapter heading in his last Morse novel, *The Remorseful Day*, in 1999.

I think my best parody is 'Homage to Betjeman', written on his death in 1984. In his superb biography of the laureate, *John Betjeman: The Bonus of Laughter* (John Murray, 2004), Bevis Hillier described it as 'probably the best of the *in memoriam* offerings at the time'.

It was followed in 1996, the centenary of A. E. Housman's classic work, by 'A Shropshire Lass', which was praised by Colin Dexter in his annual lecture to the Housman Society. These two parodies, together with eight more of my poems, have been set to music in a sequence called 'A Century of Song', which is coupled with a ceremonial march and a lyric suite for violin and piano in my CD *Fine Tuning,* released in 2008 by Da Capo Music Ltd in its 'New Century Classics' series, NCC 2006.

When Sir John Betjeman, the Poet Laureate, died in 1984 I wrote a tribute to him in the style of his 'Hymn' written in the 1930s. It was published in The Betjemanian *some years later. Like his 'Hymn', it can be sung to the tune of 'The Church's One Foundation' and was set to that music in my CD* 'Fine Tuning'.

HOMAGE TO BETJEMAN

When Betjeman departed
In nineteen-eighty-four
It left us heavy-hearted
To hear his voice no more.
His lyrical achievement
We all could understand,
And pangs of keen bereavement
Were felt throughout the land.

The comedy of manners
Was his essential strain;
Pretentious snobs and planners
Were mocked in tones urbane.
He did not seek to lecture,
But taught us to admire
Victorian architecture
In arch and roof and spire.

He carried his researches
From Cornwall to the Fens;
Great houses, villas, churches
All came before his lens.
And as he told the story
Of Salisbury or Wells
He summoned up the glory
Expressed in pealing bells.

He sang the muscled maiden,
The fragrant Surrey pines,
The cliffs with blossom laden,
Suburban railway lines.
And while a handsome station
Was lauded in his verse,
He showed that restoration
Could lead to something worse.

A morbid dread of dying
Disturbed his later years,
Though friends were always trying
To dissipate his fears.
May all his troubles cease now
Where waves assault the rock,
And may he rest in peace now
In far St Enodoc.

G. K. Chesterton's 'A Ballade of Suicide' ended on a cheerful note: 'I think I will not hang myself to-day.' My entry to a 1990 literary competition for a ballade on the theme of suicidal despair took a different view:

BALLADE OF MISERY

As Chesterton informed us long ago
The ice is breaking up on every side.
The railwaymen have voted to go slow,
The airline strikers can't be mollified.
A football team has humbled England's pride,
Our cricketers have hit a losing streak;
Two leading entertainers have just died;
I tried to kill myself three times last week.

Deep floods have followed on the heels of snow
To devastate the town where I reside;
A bolt of lightning struck my bungalow;
Two ships have foundered on the massive tide.
My maiden aunt has just been certified,
Thieves have got in and snatched my prize antique.
A maniac has stabbed a lovely bride;
I tried to kill myself three times last week.

In spirit I have never been so low,
And balk at things once taken in my stride.
When told of my redundancy, the blow
Was too much for me. I sat down and cried.
Wars and disasters flourish far and wide;
The dollar's high, the pound is up the creek,
My shares have shown a catastrophic slide;
I tried to kill myself three times last week.

My Lord, the horrors cannot be denied
Whichever way you look, the future's bleak.
The only remedy is suicide;
I tried to kill myself three times last week.

A VISION OF THE FUTURE

In 1891 J. K. Stephen wrote a stinging criticism of contemporary
writers, addressed to 'R.K.' This is how it ended:

> Will there never come a season
> Which shall rid us from the curse
> Of a prose that knows no reason
> And an unmelodious verse.
> When there stands a muzzled stripling,
> Mute, beside a muzzled bore:
> When the Rudyards cease from kipling
> And the Haggards ride no more.

In 1991 I thought I would have a shot at a parody of his work, with
a contemporary setting and a little humour.

> Could we see a situation
> Where "celebrities" are banned,
> And the swift incarceration
> Of the thugs who stalk our land.
> When the bureaucrats stop trampling
> On the rights of rich and poor;
> When the Charlottes cease from rampling,
> And the Bowleses park no more.

The centenary of Housman's A Shropshire Lad *was celebrated in 1996. This affectionate tribute to him was published by my old colleague John Julius Norwich in his annual* Christmas Cracker *and reprinted in his anthology* Still More Christmas Crackers *(Viking, 2000). In his review of that book in* The Spectator, *Sir John Mortimer praised my poem for its elegiac elegance. By this time I had set it to the music of Schubert's 'Trout' (Da Capo Music, 2000). I sent Sir John a copy of the score in the hope that he would like to try it out. He replied that he hadn't much of a voice, but he would sing it in the bath.*

A SHROPSHIRE LASS

In spring the hawthorn scatters
Its snow along the hedge,
And thoughts of country matters
Run strong on Wenlock Edge.

So fared I, loose and feckless,
And met a maiden fair;
She wore an amber necklace
To match her tawny hair.

Her mouth was soft and willing,
Her eyes were like the sea;
I offered her a shilling
If she would lie with me.

At that she blushed so sweetly
And cast her fine eyes down;
Then, whispering discreetly,
Suggested half-a-crown.

This entry in the 1997 Housman Society Poetry Competition was shortlisted, and published in the anthology Departures. *It was also read at the annual Housman Memorial Service in Ludlow Church in April 1998. John Heald, chairman of the Betjeman Society, found it very moving.*

Harold Gimblett (1914–78), a fine Somerset batsman who played for England, was barred from the Long Room at Lord's in 1977 because he was not a member of the MCC. Already sick and depressed, he died by his own hand in the following year.

A SOMERSET LAD

Harold, lad, you've hit your wicket,
Quit a life whose pitch was flat.
Once you topped the world of cricket,
Wielding high the willow bat.

Then your bronzed and brawny forearms
Rippling, smote the leathern sphere,
Till the bowlers cursed their sore arms,
And the fieldsmen fled in fear.

You were not the lad to linger,
Knew your innings would not last;
Walked before the umpire's finger
Beckoned, smiling as you passed.

Entry to the Lord's Pavilion
Can no longer be denied;
Now's your chance to make a million,
Batting on the other side.

The young lady who kissed Leigh Hunt, jumping from the chair she sat in, might have looked rather different in middle age.

JENNY AT 40

Jenny kissed me when we met,
Looking rather fat and frisky;
Rancid reek of cigarette
Mingled with the fumes of whisky.
Though I'm short of female chums
(Truth to tell, I haven't any),
When the Day of Judgement comes
Spare me Jenny!

LOVELACE BLEEDING

Don't tell me, sweet, that I'm unkind
Each time I black your eye,
Or raise a weal on your behind
I'm just a loving guy.

I love it when you scratch and bite
And leave me feeling bruised;
Unless we fought throughout the night
I wouldn't be amused.

We both despise the gentle touch,
So cut out the pretence;
You wouldn't love it half as much
Without the violence.

THE BRIGHT-EYED BRITISH IDOL

In the summer of 2009 the Ministry of Defence decided to revoke the ability of Gurkha soldiers, who had fought for Britain in many campaigns, to remain in the UK with their families. This bad decision created a national uproar, and a campaign was led by Joanna Lumley to restore their right to reside here. Given the overwhelming support for her campaign, the MOD had to climb down and allow the Gurkhas their well-deserved admission and residence.

Joanna's triumphant visit to Kathmandu reminded me of the classic monologue written by an Edwardian North Country actor, Milton Hayes, for a theatre audience: 'The Green Eye of the Yellow God', which Bransby Williams, the grand old man of the English music hall, used to recite to spine-chilling effect. It began like this:

There's a one-eyed yellow idol to the north of Kathmandu,
There's a little marble cross below the town.
There's a broken-hearted woman tends the grave of Mad Carew,
And the yellow god forever gazes down.

The opportunity for a parody seemed too good to miss, and it inspired this little tribute to 'Comely Lumley':

There's a bright-eyed British idol who has come to Kathmandu,
To a rapturous reception in that town.
She has shown a stingy Ministry the things that they can do,
And the Gurkha folk have offered her their crown.

I like to take a well-known popular song and write a revised version of the lyrics, to humorous effect if possible. The following was written in 2009, when the hapless prime minister was under attack not only from the opposition but also from members of his own party, including the cabinet. His days appeared to be numbered, and I thought it might be timely to do a little take on the Dad's Army *theme.*

THE WAR OF THE LABOUR SUCCESSION

Mr Brown had settled down in his financial den,
But came an awful cropper when he moved to No. 10.
So who do you think will be the Labour Leader
Now that Gordon's on the run?
We want to know who will win this little game,
We want to know who will save the Party's name.
So who do you think will be the Labour Leader
When old Gordon's day is done?

In September 2005 a British medical research study found that smokers have a higher risk of going blind than non-smokers due to macular degeneration. These cautionary verses, written in 2006, were put to the Royal College of Ophthalmologists as the possible theme of an anti-smoking TV advertising campaign. The idea was favourably received, but nothing came of it.

SMOKING HARMS YOUR EYES
(After Otto Harbach)

They asked me why I smoked
Till I nearly choked.
Calmly I replied
We must each decide
Risks to be defied.

They said some day you'll find
You are going blind;
When your fag's on fire
You must realise
Smoking harms your eyes.

So I laughed
And told them they were daft
To worry about my sight.
Yet today
My sight has gone away,
I am without eyesight.

Now friends make fun of me
'Cos I cannot see.
Sadder and more wise
I would strongly advise
Smoking harms your eyes.

The year 2009 saw the seventy-fifth anniversary of Cole Porter's great musical Anything Goes. *It included the memorable song 'You're the Top', in which the hapless suitor praises his beloved in extravagant terms and at inordinate length. How might this lady have responded in appropriate fashion, dismissing the chump who is so obviously inferior to her in every way?*

YOU'RE THE PITS

(After Cole Porter)

You're the pits!
You're a Nature's error.
You're the Blitz,
You're the War on Terror
You're the nasty smell of a cheap hotel in Spain,
You're the Deep Recession,
You're repossession,
You're crack cocaine.
You're a creep,
You're a pop star's worst work,
You're the sheep,
In a Damien Hirst work,
I am looked upon as the paragon of wits,
But if, baby, I'm the cherry,
You're the pits.

You're the pits,
You're a running eyesore,
You're the spits
On the streets of Mysore
You're the sick design of a Frankenstein reborn,
You're an asset stripper,
You're Jack the Ripper,
You're website porn.
You're a wimp
From a line of shirkers;
You're a pimp
With illegal workers.
I'm a lady who is invited to the Ritz,
But if, baby, I'm the cherry,
You're the pits!

This little parody was specially commissioned by John Julius Norwich for his Christmas Cracker, *published in December 2009.*

Like most of my lyrics, it was copied to my mentor, Stephen Sondheim, who wrote: 'Thanks so much for sending the lyric. It's a wonderful idea and you've done a spiffy job with it. Brilliant again!'

THE GENESIS OF 'JERUSALEM'

We're all familiar with the stirring hymn 'Jerusalem'. The ladies of the Women's Institute have the attractive habit of singing it at every opportunity; it enlivens the Last Night of the Proms; and it's increasingly used at funeral services.

The words were written 200 years ago by that great English visionary William Blake, in the preface to his monumental mythological poem *Milton*. He did not, of course, intend it as an anthem in praise of England, as it has now become; he was a proto-socialist writer who was making a clarion call to the government of the day to introduce the kind of measures needed to improve the lot of the poor and the downtrodden, and so to achieve the Christian paradise of his vision.

The music itself has an interesting history. In 1915, when the First World War was going badly for Britain, the government set up a committee of eminent writers, artists, composers and theatre people, under the chairmanship of the Poet Laureate, Robert Bridges, to consider ways of raising public morale. One of its members was his friend, Sir Hubert Parry, best known for his choral works, and Bridges asked him to set Blake's poem to music.

So it came about that on 28 March 1916, in the Queen's Hall, London, a significant event took place: the first performance of a great national song. Robert Bridges took the chair at a 'Fight for Right' rally, and in his opening address he pointed out that the object of the meeting had been perfectly expressed by the poet William Blake, who, a hundred years before, at the time of the Napoleonic Wars, wrote that inspirational poem 'Jerusalem', and equally by Parry's superb musical setting.

Another member of the committee was the famous impresario Charles Cochran. In March 1918 he put on a huge show in the Royal Albert Hall called *Fifty Years of Song* to celebrate the attainment of the final stage in the 'Votes for Women' campaign. He had decided to include 'Jerusalem' in the programme, and it made a great impression when sung by a choir with an orchestra conducted by the composer and Reginald Foort at the organ. It was subsequently adopted by the National Federation of Women's Institutes (NFWI) and has become world-famous.

When I retired from the diplomatic service in 1987 I joined the Labour Party and got in touch with Mo Mowlam, whom I had first met when she was a lecturer at Newcastle University. She had just been elected a Labour MP and had become a popular political figure. I spoke to her about the embarrassing scene at every party conference when 'The Red Flag' was sung and all the leading politicians on the platform shuffled uneasily because they did not know the words. I knew the song had been written by James M. Connell, a left-wing Irish journalist, in 1889, and had little relevance to the current Labour Party. I suggested that it would be more appropriate if the conference were to end with the singing of 'Jerusalem'. Mo liked the idea and put it to the president of the NFWI, and at subsequent conferences a WI choir has come forward and sung 'Jerusalem'.

VERSE TRANSLATION

When I started learning French, in 1938, there was a strong emphasis on the literature rather than speaking the language, and I became particularly interested in the country's poetry. My first attempt at translating verse into English was a school exercise in 1944 to produce a version of Rouget de Lisle's 1792 'Marseillaise', to celebrate the liberation of Paris.

After I retired in 1987, I reread some of my favourite poets and developed a lasting affection for the earlier ones: Charles d'Orléans, Ronsard and La Fontaine, as well as the nineteenth-century symbolists such as Baudelaire and Sully-Prudhomme. The art of Joachim du Bellay in fixing the special form of the French sonnet in the sixteenth century appealed to me. I was most impressed by the poems he wrote while in exile in Rome, a sonnet sequence called *Les Regrets* in which No. XXXI, with its air of dignified sadness, is generally regarded as the finest.

There is always a difficulty in condensing the French alexandrine into the English iambic pentameter; fortunately English has a vast number of single-syllable words that facilitate this compression. In some of the earlier poems one has also to accommodate the author's stylistic mannerisms: the inversion of the sentence, the convention of contrast, the classical allusion.

My method is to retain the original's construction, and to translate it in exactly the same form of rhyme and metre. I start by making a straightforward prose version of the text, and look for a suitable rhyme scheme. When that falls into place I turn the prose into verse. I try to use contemporary English where possible in order to capture the style as well as the meaning of the original. When the first draft is completed I put it to one side and return to it some time later to add the finishing touches. The following translation was completed in 2005.

LES REGRETS, SONNET XXXI

(Joachim du Bellay, 1522–60)

Heureux qui, comme Ulysse, a fait un beau voyage,
Ou comme cestuy la qui conquit la toison,
Et puis est retourné, plein d'usage et raison,
Vivre entre ses parents le reste de son âge!

Quand revoiray-je, hélas, de mon petit village
Fumer la cheminée, et en quelle saison
Revoiray-je le clos de ma pauvre maison,
Qui m'est une province, et beaucoup d'avantage?

Plus me plaist le séjour qu'ont basty mes ayeux
Que des palais Romains le front audacieux,
Plus que le marbre dur me plaist l'ardoise fine,

Plus mon Loyre Gaulois, que le Tybre Latin,
Plus mon petit Lyré que le mont Palatin,
Et plus que l'air marin la doulceur Angevine.

AN EXILE'S THOUGHTS OF HOME

Happy the man whose Odyssey's complete,
Or Jason-like has claimed his recompense,
Returning rich in knowledge and good sense,
To end his days in family retreat!

Ah, shall I ever see my village street,
With smoke upcurling from the chimney vents,
The courtyard of my simple residence,
More than a province in my mind's conceit?

Dearer to me is my ancestral home
Than the bold face of palaces in Rome;
Finer than marble, slate will better please,
Fairer than Tiber is that Loire of mine,
Gentler my uplands than the Palatine,
And milder Anjou air than ocean breeze.

A PASSION FOR POETRY

Like many people of my generation, I was introduced to poetry in the 1930s through the medium of hymns and popular songs – the former in Sunday school and the latter from the radio. I developed an interest in the lyrics of both, particularly such classic songs as 'Smoke Gets in Your Eyes', written in 1933. At my elementary school our English lessons included the reciting of light verse; the blinding revelation came at the local grammar school when I discovered the classic English, French and German poets. I liked Gray's 'Elegy' for its gentle melancholy and fluency, and Goldsmith's 'The Deserted Village'. The sonnet was my favourite form for its ingenious structure, and I occasionally tried to write one.

After I left the RAF in 1948 I set about making myself familiar with the work of the late Victorians – Hardy, Hopkins and Housman. I did not care for the Edwardian and Georgian poets, whose work I found rather facile and feeble, and for a time I thought the free verse of Eliot and his followers too formless. I turned to Auden (possibly the finest English poet of the twentieth century) and Betjeman (the most popular). When I began to write poems again I found it easier to work in the traditional literary forms of rhyme and metre.

For many years a peripatetic career precluded the writing of verse, but in my retirement there has been a burst of activity. More recently I have set a number of my poems to music, translated several French poets, and produced parodies of some English ones, particularly if there was an opportunity for humour. Much of this is light verse, in fact, but sometimes it achieves the intensity of 'emotion recollected in tranquillity' that true poetry must have.

70

From time to time the editor of The Betjemanian, *the annual journal of the Betjeman Society, invited members to contribute their own poems. My turn came in 2003/2004 with the following entry. I had always had an affection for the much quoted melancholic phrases of 'The Deserted Village' by the poet Oliver Goldsmith (1730–94), which inspired me to write this sonnet.*

ON AN EMPTY HOUSE

It stands, a gaunt and crumbling pile of stone,
Surrounded by a drear expanse of moor.
No mason could its former pride restore;
The elements have claimed it for their own.
The gravelled drive is thickly overgrown,
For years no man has trod inside the door.
This, the famed haunt of lords in days of yore,
Is now uncared-for, undesired, unknown.
No longer parties gather for the grouse,
Nor awe-struck tourists pay their curious call;
Where once a marquis slept reclines a mouse,
In fine apartments loathsome creatures crawl.
This dismal fate awaits a mighty house –
Today it stands; tomorrow it may fall.

As well as serious poems like 'The Song of the Shirt' and 'The Bridge of Sighs', Thomas Hood (1799–1845) wrote many humorous verses, often resorting to deft wordplay. This sonnet was an attempt to imitate his style.

TO AN OLD PAIR OF TROUSERS

Twin paragons of cunning tailor's art!
Who surely framed thee (nor his wish was vain)
E'en to amaze the world's admiring heart
That he could twice perfection thus attain.
With mingled pain and pride I pay my thanks
To thee, old friend, whose honest, sturdy cloth
Protected well these feeble spindly shanks,
Withstanding yet the ravage of the moth.
In winter's frost and tepid summer worn,
Thy sterling worth outscorned the vilest weather;
And oft, when rudely ripped by nail or thorn,
The nimble seamstress drew thy threads together.
Now ends our close attachment through the years,
Thy strength dissolved in tears, and mine in tears.

LIGHT VERSE

Although Jean Paul Getty, the billionaire philanthropist (1892–1976), entertained lavishly at Sutton Place, his Tudor manor house in Surrey, legend has it that he installed a payphone for the use of his guests. Could it be that his personal lifestyle was sometimes frugal? This verse explores one possibility.

FOR THE FALLEN

At table, J. Paul Getty was
A man of modest taste;
He dined on simple food because
He hated any waste.

He liked to have his chef prepare
A burger on a bun,
Replete with lots of gooey fare
That tends to overrun.

He wore a kind of overall
To mop up any mess,
Which, whimsically, he would call
The 'Getty's burger dress'.

A unique English literary figure of the twentieth century was the Nobel-prizewinning playwright Harold Pinter. His prolific output and distinctive personal style had a major influence on the British theatre and earned him a place in the dictionary for the term 'Pinteresque'. I thought he deserved a tribute at the time of his death on New Year's Eve in 2008.

THANKS TO PINTER

There was a fine playwright named Pinter
Whose works bore the menace of winter.
Occasional clauses
Appeared between pauses,
Which proved quite a task for the printer.

In 2009 I was inspired to write a limerick about the surfeit of repeated episodes of the TV series featuring Inspectors Frost and Morse.

TV TECS

It is Nature's immutable law,
When the weather is icy and raw,
That the loo freezes up;
But the frost eases up
And you're happy to see the john thaw.

ARTISTS' ACHIEVEMENTS

A tour of 'Art on the Côte d'Azur' in 2006 was a wonderful opportunity to visit the studios of post-Impressionist and Fauvist painters, including Renoir and Matisse. The following verse was one offshoot.

A painter named Henri Matisse,
Who had an apartment in Nice,
Abandoned his wife
For the rest of her life,
To work on his collages in peace.

* * * * *

A lesser-known Victorian painter of great ability was Atkinson Grimshaw. I'm not sure whether his skills extended to this unusual medium, but his name was irresistible.

An artist named Atkinson Grimshaw
Spent part of his time carving scrimshaw
From the teeth and the tails
Of the seals and the whales
Washed up on the Pacific Rim shore.

THE CRYPTIC CRAFT

In September 2004 I was invited to give a talk on the theme of language at the annual general meeting of the Queen's English Society. I chose to speak about the unique qualities of English which inspire fine wordplay, and the value of the cryptic crossword as an educational tool.

What is the world's favourite intellectual pastime – is it chess, bridge, mah-jongg, backgammon, Scrabble? No, it's none of these – it's solving crossword puzzles.

The crossword puzzle is one of the most universally popular inventions of the twentieth century. In Britain alone, several million people enjoy their daily dose of puzzling. It's estimated that over 80 per cent of the world's daily newspapers carry some form of crossword – as well as many weekly papers and magazines.

The crossword appears to be a combination of the old acrostics and word squares which date back to ancient Greece. The first one was devised in 1913 by Arthur Wynne, an English journalist working on the New York *Sunday World*. Looking to provide his readers with some entertainment, he composed a diamond-shaped grid with all the words interlocking and simple definition clues. He called it a 'Word-cross'.

As the diagram expanded in size, it became necessary to introduce blank squares to separate the words. But the American style of crossword has retained the system whereby all the letters in the diagram are cross-checked by intersecting words, so that solving the across clues alone would enable you to complete the puzzle. To compensate for this, there is an element of chance in finding the right answer to the definition clues. For example, 'wild animal' or 'French city' in five letters could lead to a wide range of answers. Sometimes the diagrams are made even larger, with so many clues that the solver can happily spend more time working through it.

But it wasn't until April 1924, with the publication by Simon & Shuster of the first crossword puzzle book that the craze took off. It immediately swept America and dominated social life. It got so bad that dictionaries had to be provided on trains so that commuters could do their puzzles.

A scornful editorial in the London *Times* in December 1924 noted that 'All America has succumbed to the crossword puzzle. The crossword is a menace because it is making devastating inroads on the working hours of every rank of society.' However, two months later *The Times* had to admit that the craze had 'crossed the Atlantic with the speed of a meteorological depression'.

When the crossword made its first impact on Europe in the 1920s, most countries adopted the American system of using definition clues. In England, however, the crossword evolved into a new literary form in the hands of Edward Powys Mathers. A critic, poet and translator, he came upon the crossword puzzle as soon as it arrived from America, and realised that it had infinite literary possibilities.

In his view, the existing crosswords were dull and unenterprising because the clues were tediously unimaginative definitions. How much better, he thought, to inject the elements of wordplay and wit. By blending humour and linguistic knowledge, he came up with the cryptic clue in which the actual definition of the answer is disguised, but there are subsidiary indicators to help the solver find it.

Calling himself 'Torquemada' – a notorious Grand Inquisitor of Spain – he devised a series of 'Crosswords for Riper Years' in which the solver was teased and tortured by puns, double meanings, anagrams and even verse riddles. By March 1926 he had started his famous series of fiendishly difficult puzzles in *The Observer,* which continued to his death in 1939.

He also abandoned the elementary black and white squares of the traditional crossword and invented a new grid in which the words are separated by heavy black lines or 'bars'. The bar grid is now used by setters of the most difficult crosswords.

While Torquemada established the style of the cryptic crossword puzzle which other compilers have followed, he did not always adhere to the ground rules of fairness and accuracy. These were laid down as rigid standards by 'Afrit'– Alistair Ferguson Ritchie, headmaster of Wells Cathedral School – who started composing crosswords for the weekly *Listener.* Like Torquemada, he leaned heavily on literary allusions and classical references entailing much research. His aim, however, was not merely to test the solver's knowledge but also to entertain.

At *The Observer,* Torquemada was succeeded by three compilers, one of whom was Derrick Macnutt, senior classics master at Christ's Hospital School. He adopted the pseudonym of 'Ximenes', the cardinal who followed the original Torquemada as leader of the Spanish Inquisition. In 1945 he took over sole responsibility for the *Observer* crossword, and baffled solvers every week until his untimely death in 1971. He instituted a monthly competition in which solvers had to provide their own clue to a particular word in the diagram.

The clues submitted were marked by Ximenes like examination papers and the results circulated to all the entrants. A trophy was passed from one winner to the next. On the occasion of his 500th puzzle in September 1958, I had the honour of organising a celebration dinner at the Café Royal for his fans.

Ximenes was succeeded by Jonathan Crowther, an editor at the Oxford University Press. Searching for a suitable pseudonym, he found another Spanish Inquisitor called Don Diego de Deza. He instantly realised that Deza could be reversed to 'Azed', and that is the name that has appeared on his crossword since 1972. His 1,000th puzzle, achieved in mid-1991, was celebrated by a grand luncheon at St Hugh's College, Oxford, attended by such noted solvers as Colin Dexter, creator of the crossword-loving Inspector Morse, and Sir Jeremy Morse, whose name he borrowed. The names of other Azed solvers crop up as characters throughout the Morse mysteries.

The Times itself held out as long as it could, but in the end it bowed to public pressure and published its first crossword on 1 February 1930. It was one of the first daily papers to move away from the simple definition type of clue and introduce the 'cryptic' one, which has to be unravelled before the solver can arrive at the right answer. Its diamond jubilee in 1990 was marked with great celebrations and worldwide coverage, and in 2007 it was voted one of the ten British icons of the twentieth century. The annual *Times* National Crossword Championship, begun in 1970, attracts up to 20,000 entrants, and the final is a most exciting event as the keenest minds in the country work through six puzzles against the clock. Although it is not the hardest of its kind, its consistent qualities of sophisticated wordplay and sly humour have won it a reputation as the most famous crossword in the world. It frequently features in novels, plays and films where the author wishes to establish a brainy character. It is no coincidence that many of the British code-breakers in World War II were crossword experts.

As for solvers, when he was shouldering an incredible burden as deputy prime minister, Clement Attlee relaxed off duty with the *Times* crossword. He was even seen solving one at the Yalta Conference in 1945. Actors would often be found tackling the puzzle in their dressing room prior to going on stage. Felix Aylmer was one of the best.

Why should the cryptic crossword have developed only in English? As far as I know, you won't find it in any other language. I would hazard a guess that, although it originated as recently as the 1920s, it stems from the British love of word games that were so popular as family entertainment in Victorian England, and from the work of such writers as Edward Lear and Lewis Carroll. The latter even used linguistic wordplay to construct his pen-name: 'Charles' became 'Carroll' and 'Lutwidge' became 'Lewis'. What a clever 'Dodge, son'!

Then the 1920s was a period when the country house party was at its height, and it was customary for people to settle down to charades and pencil-and-paper games after dinner. Torquemada picked up this tradition and translated it into the crossword.

Secondly, the English language has evolved over time as a melting pot of words derived from many sources. In addition to the Romance and North European languages which form the basis of the English tongue, there are the words brought back by Britons from the former colonies, infusions from Chinese and Russian, contributions from Turkish and Arabic. Greek provides the basis of political thought, science and technology; Latin, of religion, medicine and the arts.

English has eagerly taken in everything. Consequently the language contains many words with multiple meanings, deriving from completely different roots, or complete opposites: thus 'cleave' can mean to split apart or to adhere strongly, and 'resign' could be to leave a job or to continue in it. And it is not uncommon for a single word like 'round' to serve as noun, verb, adverb, adjective and preposition. These ambiguities are seized upon by crafty crossword compilers who manipulate the language to confuse and mislead the solver.

Thirdly, the English language is unique in possessing so many short words which can be used to make up longer ones to which they are in no way related. Take the word 'insignificant', for example. It breaks down neatly into 'in-sign-if-I-can't'. Or 'refrigerator', which becomes 'ref-rig-era-tor'. Tricks of this kind are the meat and drink of crossword compilers. One of the most sophisticated practitioners of this form of literary fun saw that 'brainwash' may be broken down as 'bra-in-wash' and clued as 'bust down reason'.

Anagrams are no longer indicated by 'anag' in brackets, but by words in the clue suggesting confusion, error, drunkenness, building, possibility, and so on. Thus, 'The President *saw nothing* wrong' may be construed as 'Washington'. Taking this to its highest form, the whole clue becomes a definition of the answer, as in '*Thing called* shaky illumination?', giving 'candlelight'.

Then there are many instances of one word slipped inside another to make a third, as in 'ca(bare)t', 'come(lines)s' and 'th(ink)ing'. Juxtapositions abound: 'late-rally', 'Inca-hoots', 'rein-for-cement'. Or a word can be hidden in the clue: for example, 'Prime Minister seen in the Athenaeum' gives 'Heath'.

Another popular device is homophones – words that sound alike. 'Wales', 'whales' and 'wails' are typical of this kind. In some cases a foreign import can sound like an English word: the rubber substance 'gutta-percha' becomes the street urchin 'gutter-percher'. The crossword compiler has all these tricks up his sleeve, and many more. His tool is the English language in its infinite flexibility, and he uses it to baffle the solver in a devious but entertaining fashion.

I'm not a teacher of English, but I believe that crosswords could have a special educational value in teaching spelling, improving vocabulary and extending general knowledge at the primary level. Later the more complex type could help to sharpen the mental process, encourage the use of reference works, and show how our wonderful language has evolved – and all this through what is an enjoyable game. I should like to see crosswords introduced in schools as part of the literacy programme.

4 August, 1970

Many congratulations on winning the Crossword
Championship.

I knew that there were many quick-witted and well-read
people in the Service but it was good to see this so
widely advertised in the papers yesterday.

(ALEC DOUGLAS-HOME)

C. R. Dean, Esq.

THE RIGHT SETTING

The Foreign and Commonwealth Office Association of retired British diplomats was formed in 1999. As a link with members it published a magazine called *Password*. The editor asked me to contribute a cryptic crossword of a reasonable standard. I was happy to do this, and over the years I set twenty-five crosswords of a kind which readers seemed to like. My final puzzle was published in 2010. I had taken the pseudonym 'Diplodocus' for my work because, unlike all the other setters of my acquaintance, I did not possess the computer which makes it possible to fill in a given grid very quickly. My puzzles were made by a more primitive method and a Stone Age name seemed appropriate.

In 2002 I was invited to set crosswords for the *Church Times*, a weekly newspaper with excellent coverage of foreign affairs. I had to be careful to include a number of clues and words with some religious connections in each puzzle, which did not come easily to me. However, I clocked up twenty-four of these before retiring in 2009.

In 2003 I received the ultimate accolade of joining the team of setters of the *Times* crossword, which is recognised as having the highest standard of any daily paper. Over the next seven years I set forty-one cryptic crosswords for the paper, usually on a Monday. On my eightieth birthday I was given the honour of a puzzle devised by the crossword editor, celebrating my life and career – the first and only time a living person has been so honoured. As my mental faculties diminished I decided to withdraw in 2010. My last puzzle had the theme of retirement and was published on my eighty-third birthday.

PUZZLES IN THE UNDERGROUND
(The Answer Lies at the End of the Line)

For some years Transport for London (TFL) has operated a project called 'Art on the Underground', in which commercial advertisements in the carriages of the Tube network are enlivened here and there by paintings, photographs or poems, giving passengers the opportunity to look at something attractive or amusing, and thus alleviate the boredom of a journey.

In 2008 TFL had the bright idea of introducing crosswords. Stanmore was chosen as the base because the town housed a wartime outstation of the code-breakers at Bletchley Park, many of whom had been recruited for their ability to solve cryptic crosswords. I was invited to give a hand in setting up the operation, in collaboration with eight local groups and organisations who had an interest in crosswords. I took part in a seminar in Stanmore and supplied comments on their own puzzles.

The project was developed by the artist Serena Korda, who created a number of magnificent paintings on the ceiling of the booking hall in which the crossword grids were encircled by heraldic designs. My portrait featured in a poster on the station platform, and my own crossword grid appeared on the cover of a booklet containing eight crosswords which passengers picked up as they boarded a train at the station – the end of the Jubilee Line – so that they could try to solve them on the journey. 'Crosswords on the Underground' ran from July 2008 to January 2009, and had a great success with the public.

The following piece of pedantry was inspired by a series of serious grammatical errors in the English media in 2006. It was first published in Quest, *the journal of the Queen's English Society, in summer 2007. Sadly, the state of ignorance has since grown worse.*

VERBAL ABUSE

There seems to be some confusion in the media about the conjugation of irregular verbs of Germanic origin using the vowel 'i'. Recent examples are: "as the news sunk in", "they rung the bell", "the choir sung" and "he swum the channel".

The confusion may arise from the fact that many of the Germanic verbs we have inherited conjugate irregularly for no apparent reason. Some of them follow the German pattern of vowel changes to 'a' in the imperfect tense and 'u' in the past participle: 'begin', 'drink', 'ring', 'shrink', 'sing', 'sink', 'spring', 'stink' and 'swim'. Others keep the vowel change to 'u' in both the imperfect tense and the past participle: cling, fling, sling, slink, spin, sting, swing and wring.

(Another verb whose forms are often misused is 'run', which belongs to the 'a' and 'u' family).

Then there are the odd ones that mutate into a vowel other than 'u' in the imperfect tense and past participle; 'win' and 'shine' go for 'O', while 'bind', 'find', 'grind' and 'wind' prefer 'ou', as do 'bring' and 'think', which approximate most closely to the German pattern by changing the consonants as well as the vowels.

This may be a small grammatical point, but it is important to get it right if people are to speak and write properly. If grammar is still taught in our schools, it might be a good idea for teachers to set simple sentence exercises designed to show the different ways in which these irregular verbs are conjugated.

My interest in words extends to the invention of new ones. This collection was published in Quest *in summer 2008.*

BRAVE NEW WORDS

I've read in *The Times*, and heard on BBC Radio 4, that the search is on for new words in the English language worthy of inclusion in the dictionary. As a writer myself, I have a special interest in this subject, and I've submitted some of my own coinage (which has been published in various places) to the major lexicographers. Sadly, none of them has yet found favour with the authorities.

Frauditor
This word first appeared in my letter to *The Times* of 17 February 1988: "I believe that the English language is flexible enough to accommodate new words to describe new developments. In the field of economics, I suggest: Frauditor (n) one who investigates financial irregularities."

My word was used by the *Economist* on 11 December 1988, in ITN News on 15 December 1988, and possibly elsewhere. It then gained an entry in *The Longman Register of New Words,* Volume Two, 1990, as follows: "The word 'frauditor' in the sense of 'defrauder, cheat' (which is 'fraudator' in Latin), was used over 400 years ago, in Thomas Wilson's *Art of Rhetoric,* 1553. But this is not related to Mr Dean's coinage – a blend of, 'fraud' and 'auditor'– which appears to have caught on, at least temporarily. It is used particularly in the context of vetting share applications for newly privatised companies, to make sure that each individual submits only one."

Freudenschade
I had been trying for some years, in letters to the press, to get this useful word accepted. It finally made it in the correspondence column of the *Observer* on 31 December 2006, under the heading 'Ode to Shameful Joy': "The Comment by Christina Odone (Hurrah for those real-life panto moments, 17 December) and letter from

Werner Krupps (last week) on 'schadenfreude', reminded me that there is no single word to express a feeling of disappointment at somebody else's success. I suggest 'Freudenschade' might fill the gap."

Clericks
The chief glory of the clerihew, invented by E. C. Bentley in 1905, is that the lines are of uneven length and do not scan. Perversely, the 'clerick', invented by me in 1997, takes an existing clerihew, adjusts the wording to fit a metre, and adds a fifth line in the style of a limerick. Here is one example:

> To his servant said Christopher Wren
> I am going to dine with some men.
> If anyone calls,
> I'm designing St. Paul's,
> So please ask them to call back again.

Decouplets
This word was also coined in 1997 as an appropriate term for the game or competition in which you have to take a well-known line of verse and add an incongruous rhyming line to achieve a bathetic effect, as these examples show:

> This is the Night Mail crossing the border,
> Hoping the signals are now in order.

> Unkempt about these hedges blows
> A filthy tramp his streaming nose.

> Grow old along with me
> In pensioned poverty.

> Go and catch a falling star
> Who's had too many at the bar.

> I know a bank whereon the wild thyme grows;
> You can't get money there – it's had to close.

Trimericks

The limericks of Edward Lear are somewhat disappointing since the fifth line ends with the same word as the first. All his successors have used rhyme throughout, which achieves a greater impact.

The 'Trimerick' is a new type of verse in the form of a limerick, but instead of rhyming, the three long lines end in homophones. Here are the first examples:

> There was an old man of Toulouse
> Whose house was equipped with two loos.
> He said to his son
> "I shall get rid of one,
> Because I have nothing to lose."

> A helpful curator at Kew,
> On seeing the length of the queue,
> Said "I'll open the gate
> So you won't have to wait."
> And they entered, precisely on cue.

> An alchemist working at Tintern
> In his search for a way to make tin turn
> Into goods to be sold,
> Found by painting it gold,
> Much more would the bright yellow tint earn.

> There was a young fellow from Wales
> Who liked to go hunting for whales;
> Till a clumsy buffoon
> Struck him with a harpoon;
> How terrible then were his wails!

WORD-ROW REVIVER DEIFIED

From my early youth I had been interested in the structure of words. Reversals like 'deliver' and 'reviled' appealed to me, until I discovered palindromes – the perfect reflections. This piece about my hobbyhorse was written in 1998.

Palindromes can be traced back as far as ancient Greece; according to Brewer, their reputed inventor was Sotades, a scurrilous Greek poet of the third century BC. The word itself comes from the Greek *palindromos*, meaning 'running back again'. Since a palindrome is a word or line reading the same both ways, the most appropriate definition would be 'word-row', though this useful term does not seem to have interested the lexicographers so far.

The English language is rich in single-word palindromes. The repetition of the consonant makes them the easiest words for a child to say, hence the names for parents: 'mum' (dialect 'mam' and US *'mom'*), 'dad' and 'pop'. And a grandmother is 'nan'.

Extreme vowels in three-letter palindromes are also fairly common, but do not strike the ear so readily. There is a remarkable sequence with the letter 'e'– 'ere', 'eve', 'ewe', 'Exe', 'eye'– in which the sound of the vowel is entirely dependent on the middle consonant.

Words with an odd number of letters are the most frequent, since they balance nicely on the middle letter. There is an underlying significance about words like 'level' (straight in both directions) and those indicating some kind of turning movement, as in 'radar', 'rotor', 'rotator' and 'rotavator'.

Attempts have been made to coin even longer palindromic words.

The best is the eleven-letter chemical formation 'detartrated'– free of tartaric acid. Finnish goes one better with 'saippua-kauppias'– a soap seller.

The perfect word-row would be a line constructed from individual palindromes, as in the mediaeval Latin example: *"Anna tenet mappam, madidam mappam tenet Anna."* But this does not seem possible in English.

It is, however, possible to manipulate a number of word reversals to form a palindromic line. The earliest in English appears to be one coined by Phillips in 1706: "Lewd did I live, & evil I did dwel" – though the ampersand is a bit of a cop-out. Napoleon did better with his comment (through his interpreter?): "Able was I ere I saw Elba."

A modern example is: "No gateman sniper repins nametag on," which conjures up a picture of a shooting incident at the entrance to a factory involving a homicidal custodian wishing to conceal his identity.

When it comes to free-flowing palindromic sentences, English is undoubtedly the richest language, by virtue of its variety of sources and its flexibility.

The most familiar is the remark attributed to the first man in the Garden of Eden, introducing himself to his lady (in English, naturally): "Madam, I'm Adam." She could have replied, pointing out that she is unmarried: "Eve, Miss – I'm Eve." A later biblical example is Noah's query to his helmsman: "Was it Ararat I saw?"

In the latter part of the nineteenth century, word games became a popular family pastime, instigated by such experts as Edward Lear and Lewis Carroll. An American doctor named Charles Bombaugh published a collection of *Gleanings for the Curious from the Harvest Fields of Literature,* edited by Martin Gardner as *Oddities and Curiosities of Words and Literature* (Dover, 1961). It includes such ingenious palindromes as: "Now stop, major-general, are negro jampots won?" and "Stiff, O dairyman, in a myriad of fits".

More recently, there is this splendid effort by Peter Hilton, a British mathematician working as a code-breaker at Bletchley Park during the Second World War: "Doc, note I dissent. A fast never prevents a fatness. I diet on cod.'

The greatest of modern palindromists is J. A. Lindon. In 1976 he composed an ingenious dialogue between Adam and Eve (reproduced by John Julius Norwich in his *Christmas Cracker* for 1993). Their union concluded with Adam's rapturous statement: "Diamond-eyed no-maid!"

Lindon may also have been the author of that acute observation: "Sex at noon taxes." On reflection (which one must always do with palindromes), one could visualise a matching piece of advice to lovers to complete the proverb: "Six a.m. – maxis!".

Another fine palindromist working in the 1950s was Leigh Mercer. He is author of this brilliant summary of a civil engineering feat: "A man, a plan, a canal – Panama!" Mercer may have been a schoolmaster, for his other well-known line is the academic dictum: 'Sums are not set as a test on Erasmus."

Burton Bernstein, biographer of Thurber, and younger brother of Leonard grew up in a household where wordplay dominated the conversation. Burton's major contribution to the art of the palindrome is a playlet entitled "Look, Ma, I Am Kool!", published in his collection of casual pieces (Prentice-Hall, 1977).

Some apposite phrases stay in the mind. One that should appeal to gardeners is: "Goldenrod adorned log." For teachers: "Pupils slip up." For music-lovers: "If I had a hi fi." And for a motorist's rear window: "Pull up if I pull up!"

Perhaps the time has come to revive the palindrome as a literary form. Some years ago it occurred to me that one way to stimulate interest would be to compose a poem in which every line was a palindrome. Although writing palindromic verse is incredibly time-consuming, particularly if it has to rhyme and scan, some enjoyable nonsense can be produced. Now and again some kind of meaning begins to emerge, as in this couplet:

> Sleepless evening, nine. Vessel peels;
> Sleek cats yell at alley, stack eels.

These are the opening lines of 'Senile's Reverie i' Reverse Lines', an atmospheric poem in six stanzas describing the scene in a seedy American waterfront bar, seen through the eyes of an elderly drunk.

In his fascinating book Language on Vacation (Scribner's, 1965) Professor Dmitri Borgmann challenged anyone to write a palindromic poem. This effort, the ramblings of an elderly drunk in a seedy waterfront bar on the East coast of America, took twenty years to produce. It was published in John Julius Norwich's anthology More Christmas Crackers (Penguin, 1992), and is believed to be the longest palindromic poem in English.

SENILE'S REVERIE I' REVERSE LINES

I

Sleepless evening, nine. Vessel peels;
Sleek cats yell at alley, stack eels.
Rabelais, send a sadness! I, ale-bar,
Rajah sahib at tab, I hash a jar.
Burton, odd nap, I sip and do not rub,
But liven as partner entraps an evil tub.
No, it's a bar, ever a bastion;
No ill imbibe, not one. Bib million,
Zillion US pints. If fist nip sun-oil, Liz,
Sit right, or free beer froth-girt is.
Red neb – a nostril – flirts on a bender,
Red net rabbi rose, so rib bartender.

II

'Netta Delia' sailed at ten;
Niagara, fall afar again.
Re-rack sack, can snack, cask-carer;
A rare Medoc! O Demerara!
Murder noses on red rum,
Mum, it poses optimum.
To predicate, go get a cider pot,
Toll a renegade, bed a general lot
To claret. Alas, it is a lateral cot

Warren, slip a Pilsner raw,
Ward, regale me, lager draw;
Walter, aback sir, I risk cabaret law.

III

Night, ninth gin.
Nip ale, lap in;
Malt some most lam.
Marc in I cram,
Gorge, niff of fine grog.
Gong! Get at egg-nog.
Too hot to hoot?
Too tall a toot
To order a red root.
Tosspot tops sot
To pay a pot,
Totes in a reviver – anise tot.

IV

Retsina, call a canister;
Ruffino pull upon. If fur,
Laminate pet animal.
Laid rock, lime-milk cordial,
Dude potion sees. No, I tope dud
Dubonnet forever, often. No, bud,
No Campari. Did I rap Macon?
No net's a fillip. Ill, I fasten on
Yale belt. To bag a bottle, belay
Yard aside. Repapered is a dray.
Martini redder in it ram;
Madeira ewer. I tire, wearied am.

V

'S midnight, flew. Twelfth gin dims;
Smirnoff – it's put up, stiff on rims.
Dray, pull up yard,
Draught nets tenth guard.
Set ale, drawn inward, elates
Set at serener estates.
No garden, I left it. Feline dragon,
No gal faster frets a flagon.
Dial simple hero, more help mislaid
Diaper motto by baby bottom repaid.
Bilge, be mildewed, lime be glib,
Bird imitators rot a timid rib.

VI

Barcarolle, clever revel. Cell or a crab?
Bar delay alerts a wastrel; a Yale drab
Tastes sop, wolfs nuts. Tuns flow possets at
Tart, nor fret away a waterfront rat.
Spill a cold image, keg amid local lips,
Spirits assent. I witness Asti rips.
Strap on gateman's name-tag. No parts
Straddle if I'd roll. Lord, I field darts,
E'en knots erotic. I to rest on knee;
Emotion's sensuousness, No.1 to me.
Pacer in mutual autumn, I recap
Pals as reviled, so red-eyed Eros delivers a slap.

MODERN SPOONERISMS

The English language has expanded greatly since the days of the Reverend W. A. Spooner (1844–1930), warden of New College, Oxford, who was noted for transposing the initial letters of the words in a phrase, possibly owing to absent-mindedness. The classic utterances attributed to him include "The Lord is a shoving leopard", "You have tasted a whole worm" and "I came here by the town drain".

There have been several competitions over the years in which entrants were asked to imitate Spooner's habit of transposition with humorous effect. Here are some of my own.

Music has Brahms to soothe a savage chest.

You need a burly chassis to belt out that song.

Matron took her exam in the knowledge of cursing.

The thief cut his hand on a blazer raid.

I had to leave the room hurriedly, being shaken taut.

Trying to save time, the driver found a court shut.

A good hotel shouldn't allow rock coaches in.

Tom goes out more now that he has a flat cap.

It's best to avoid a road that's full of hot poles.

At a formal dance the bitter jug would be banned.

My postman's pleased with the better locks I've had fitted.

Evading the defenders, he made a great Dutch town.

I'd like these shoes to be holed and sealed.

The party was quiet until two crate gashers arrived.

It's not a fair election if you keep moving the poll ghosts.

My son likes hot dogs and not poodles.

The MFH disapproved of the ladies' hiding rabbits.

Only the keenest ecologists sign up to preen geese.

You don't need a hedge slammer to crack a nut.

Having paid for the son, he dangled in the water.